Antiphilosophical Dictionary

Peter Naur

Antiphilosophical Dictionary

Thinking - Speech - Science/Scholarship

With a Summary

Med Dansk Resumé

naur♪com publishing

Antiphilosophical Dictionary
Thinking - Speech - Science/Scholarship

Cover painting: Evening Promenade in the Outskirts of Paradise, Albert Naur, 1960.

Printed in Denmark

ISBN 87-987221-1-5

Published by

naur.com publishing
Begoniavej 20
DK 2820 Gentofte
Denmark

Information about ordering can be found at the Internet home page: 'www.naur.com'.

Preface

Judging from what is called philosophy, nonsense must be among the sturdiest plants there are. The seed was sown by Aristotle 350 years B.C., and since then the philosophical nonsense has thrived. A seedling of the plant, Aristotle's talk of motion, died around 1650, but the main stem flowers unscathed today.

In this sturdiness of nonsense there is nothing inexplicable, psychologically. As noted by William James a hundred years ago (see the dictionary article *reality*), we all tend to believe what we are told or read, as long as it does not flatly contradict something in which we are currently engaged. In a debate which does not deal with matters of our special concern we all tend to agree with the latest honourable speaker. This habitual trust in speech and print again is in line with our trust in the way we perceive our ordinary surroundings, our closest fellow beings and the things, the light, and the sounds we encounter. Long periods may elapse between our experience of being astonished or frightened at something we are exposed to. Most of the time we may perceive our impressions in our habitual way, without running into surprises.

Thus it is quite understandable that when we encounter statements concerning issues at the limit of our normal field of interest, that is questions we have had hardly any occasion to give any thought, then we will tend strongly to accept them in the manner children have to accept anything they meet, uncritically. In this field we find, among other things, philosophy.

Another relevant circumstance is the general urge to know better. This urge differs from one person to another, like any other characteristic, but it is evidently lively in many people. Such people will be attracted to Aristotle's philosophical program of the highest knowledge. Philosophy, in other words, is presumption incarnate.

To this is added in recent years the commercialization of science in the form of what is called research projects. Such projects are financed on the basis of, not results, but plans. Those who grant the money and those who receive it have a common interest in defending the projects, whether or not they build upon nonsense, and the more costly the project the greater the defence interest. Disclosure of nonsense in this context thus becomes a subversive activity, in which only those can allow themselves to engage who have given up their chance of getting access to research money. Thus in research contexts nonsense thrives practically unabated.

Scientists are mostly uninterested in what philosophers say. Thus the scientists for hundreds of years, unconcerned with the philosophers' presumption, have been formulating ever more adequate and coherent descriptions of the ways of the world.

Most of those who have even glanced at what philosophers say have been puzzled to notice how the philosophers have talked for several thousand years, without being able to display a single specimen of what they say they seek: a truth.

A few scientists have joined the philosophers' club of presumption. However, if one looks close into what they say one finds that they just confirm the basic impossibility of philosophy.

The following notes are the results of irritation over the philosophical inanity accumulated over many years. The first incentive to them came from my study of what is said in philosophical texts about science, induced by my work in astronomy around 1955. Thus I came across Bertrand Russell's essay *On the Notion of Cause* (for more about this, see *cause*). His starting point is a detailed, critical analysis of what is said about causes in Baldwin's *Dictionary of Psychology and Philosophy*. In his analysis Russell shows that what is said in the handbook is unclear and self-contradictory. Russell then contrasts this philosophical confusion with the way the things are talked about in scientific astronomy, the field of my insight at first hand.

In later years my work in computing has given me the occasion to evaluate what is said in philosophical and psychological writings about people's mental activity and their perception of their surroundings and of linguistic expressions. Here I have time and again found new examples of philosophical confusion of the kind Russell indicated. However, I have never found other analyses like Russell's, and Russell himself appears in his later writings to have forgotten his antiphilosophical contribution.

The following antiphilosophical notes are primarily arranged alphabetically by subject keyword, but there are connections in all directions between the subjects, as indicated by references. No completeness has been attempted, in view of the amount of philosophical nonsense that has appeared in print. The principal views are presented in some longer articles, of which may be specially mentioned (alphabetically) *association, concept, description, feeling, knowing, language, language-rule-fallacy, perception, reality, scientific-scholarly activity, stream of thought, word-as-code-of-meaning-fallacy.*

So as to make the points of attack specific, the notes include detailed analyses of passages from selected philosophical writings. Predominantly the authors chosen are among those who have enjoyed wide international recognition, although with due regard to the local Danish scene. Lexical information, such as dates of the works or persons who are referred to, is only given exceptionally, since such information is readily available in many handbooks. The sources of the quotations and of the *Dictionary of Philosophy* I have consulted is given in a Literature Appendix. Here is also given references to such places in my other writings where I have discussed some of the views presented in the dictionary in more detail.

In choosing linguistic expressions I have aimed solely at achieving clarity: clarity in what is being talked about and clarity in what is being said about it. Thus I have made use of all the possibilities of the written form of expression, its letters and signs, its typographical variants, the way the text may be arranged in lines and paragraphs and organized with the aid of key words, in the way I find most clear in the context. In my striving for clarity I have found it necessary to ignore the concern for those styles that some people like to call correct language (about this see the article on *language-rule-fallacy*). I also ignore the aura of respect that usually is seen to enshroud philosophical statements.

At closer look most (all?) philosophy may be seen to be centered around a small handful of eternally repeated locutions that in philosophical contexts are taken to be meaningful outside of any context, typically *essence, existence, reality*. While collecting the notes I noticed a common line in all the philosophical twaddle: it goes straight back to Aristotle. While Aristotle's talk of motion was put to rest by Galileo more than 300 years ago, Aristotle still thrives in philosophy. Other general features of the philosophical talk: nonsense, more particularly elaborate talk about indefinite, misty subjects; further, poor understanding of the human mental activity, including adherence to fallacies about the linguistic activity (see *language-fallacy*). The poor understanding of the mental activity goes in parallel with the sick state of psychology, particularly in the twentieth century, the decay of psychology under the tyranny of behaviorism.

At first sight it might seem to be of no consequence that a small group of philosophers are talking nonsense. But philosophy has harmful effects far beyond the circle of philosophers. In one direction it is destructive to the general understanding of how defensible expression is constituted, that the philosophical nonsense is hailed as the highest wisdom. In another direction philosophers have taken upon themselves the highest insight into science and scholarship, and have with their talk of truth, logic, and methods, corrupted the understanding of science. This harmful influence is felt particularly in psychology. Here the philosophical fallacies about science have led to behaviorism, whereby the psychologists have cut themselves off from talking about what ought to be the center of the subject, the thoughts and feelings we all experience.

For excellent help with criticism of drafts of the book I am very grateful to Erik Frøkjær. For criticism of the English version I am greatly indebted to my sons, Jesper and Thorkil Naur.

Dictionary

Acquaintance, knowing by: Even though the philosophers who talk about knowledge seem not to have noticed it, any talk about knowing has to start by establishing that, whatever it is, knowing is inextricably tied to acquaintance. The beginning of any insight into something is to be acquainted with that something. With certain very common aspects of the world we never get much further. Thus e.g. the color blue. A person may be acquainted with the color blue, and may point to things around that are blue. But who knows anything much about the color blue?

A mental object (see *stream of thought*) is acquainted with something that is different from itself. For example, my stream of thought of a moment ago has held a mental object which is acquainted with an event that took place in November 1937: that concert at which Shostakovitch's 5th symphony was performed for the first time. Additionally, in its fringe, the mental object has something I know about that event: among other things that the listeners were so impressed at the slow movement that many of them wept; the applause after the symphony lasted longer than the symphony itself.

Acquaintance is an immediate *feeling* in the mental object. As said by William James, the relation between a mental object and that with which the object is acquainted is the most mysterious thing in the world.

The philosophers' lack of interest in acquaintance most likely is closely related to their adoration of logic. When talking about knowing *about* something it makes sense to ask whether what one knows is correct or wrong, whether what one says about it is true or false. Thus to the question: 'how long did the applause after the first performance of Shostakovitch's 5th symphony last' one may to a certain extent talk about a correct or true answer. But to ask whether my acquaintance with the first performance of Shostakovitch's 5th symphony is correct or true makes no sense.

See also *knowing*.

Aristotle: The talk about *philosophy, logic,* and *truth,* mostly goes back to Aristotle (about 350 years B.C.). His work *On Philosophy*, which survives only in fragments, is summarized in Encyclopedia Britannica thus:

'In the extant part, Aristotle defines the specific role of the philosopher. Dividing the historical development of civilization into five main stages, Aristotle sees the emergence of philosophy as its culmination. First, men are compelled to devote themselves to the creation of the necessities because without them they could not survive. Next come the arts that refine life and then the discovery of the art of politics, the prerequisite of the good life as Aristotle conceived it. To these necessities and refinements of life is added the knowledge of their proper use in the fourth stage. Only with the emergence of the well-regulated state comes the leisure for intellectual adventure, used at first for the study of the material causes of existing things. Finally comes the shift from natural to divine philosophy, when the mind lifts itself above the material world and grasps the formal and final causes of things, realizing the intelligible aspects of reality and the purpose that informs all change.'

Aristotle's notion of philosophy was directly related to the antique order of society, which built upon the division into free men and slaves. Philosophy was the speculation of the free men, with disdain for all practical activities, which were left for the slaves. Aristotle's program defines philosophy to be presumption incarnate.

Aristotle's way of talking about things dominated Western thinking for two thousand years. It had a profound influence upon the pursuit of science in antiquity, which as said by Benjamin Farrington in *Greek Science* was virtually paralyzed. In the Middle Ages the Church adopted Aristotle as being unassailable. Not until about 300 years ago was Aristotle shaken on his pedestal, when after a fierce conflict, mostly fought by *Galileo Galilæi,* Aristotle's way of talking about motion was found useless. It is astonishing that so long time had to elapse before Aristotle's nonsense in this field could be rejected, as it may be exposed in five minutes by any child. Aristotle claimed that a heavy body falls more quickly to the ground than a light one, which is easy to test. Just find two small stones of different sizes, a light one and a heavy one, and let them go at the same moment from a suitable height so as to fall upon something that makes a sound when a stone hits, e.g. a metal lid. And then listen whether there are two clicks.

The rejection of Aristotle's impossible talk about motion opened a thoroughgoing revolution in the description of our surroundings and became the beginning of modern science. But in philosophy Aristotle, in particular his talk about logic and truth, is the unchallenged ruler until today.

See *association, cause, Descartes, essence, foundations, knowing, logic, mathematical analysis, philosophy, psychology, rationality, reality, truth.*

Artificial intelligence: The talk of artificial intelligence is a fresh shoot from the Aristotelian plant, the kind of philosophical babble that at any time will teach us what we human beings *are,* what is the *essence* of a human being. Aristotle told us that we are rational animals. Descartes said that man is a soul in a machine. When the digital computers had been invented Turing immediately could talk about machines that think. Since then philosophers have spoken reverently about the great new insight, artificial intelligence. Those who say they work in artificial intelligence have not restrained their predictions that very soon—it is just on the doorstep—they will present us with a superintelligent computer. We have now had this gabble repeated over the last 40 years with no visible result. So we have to make do with machines that play chess, if that is what we need, and something the sales people call intelligent terminals.

Artificial intelligence is pursued by people having philosophical ideas, who thus in the typical manner of philosophers lack even the most primitive understanding of how the mental activity of people in fact takes place. Characteristically is it claimed in the Aristotelian style that 'man *is* an information processor'. No notice is taken of the fact that as a description of a person the information processor is miserable. People are entirely incapable of that at which an information processor is supreme: repeating the same action indefinitely. While the computer is totally unable to describe the core of mental activity, the *stream of thought, concepts,* and *association,* qq.v.

Some artificial intelligence builds upon the *thinking-as-language-fallacy,* q.v. Another branch talks about problem solving, without a sound understanding of *reasoning,* q.v. *Perception* (q.v.) is claimed to take place according to Russell's defective notion. There is much meaningless talk about representation of *knowledge* (q.v.). It is claimed that human *know-how* (q.v.) may be described in terms of rules of behavior.

See also *psychology, language-as-something-fallacy.* Further references are given in the Literature Appendix.

Association: The word association has been used since antiquity for describing the way our thoughts change from one moment to the next, and more specifically about the way the contents of our thoughts at one moment are connected to those of the next. The starting point of the talk of the association of thoughts is the introspective observation anyone may make, that the contents of thought, while changing always remain connected. One object of thought is replaced habitually by the next. We say then that the two thoughts are associated or that the next thought appears through its association to the first one.

Already Aristotle discussed that in memory recall one thought leads to another, with which in the person's previous experience it has become associated, and mentioned that thoughts may be associated by their similarity, contrast, and contiguity.

Locke maintained that thoughts may be understood as composed of elementary ideas, a kind of thought atoms, and spoke of the association of ideas. This manner of talking was adopted by several generations of English philosophers, John Stuart Mill among others.

The talk of association was taken over by William James in his classical *Principles of Psychology,* but only after a decisive revision, in James's word, a correction of a huge error, to wit, the talk of elementary ideas. As stressed by James the talk of elementary 'ideas', which should form the contents of our thoughts, is entirely untenable in view of what we may discover introspectively. Thus what enters into the association of thoughts is not elementary 'ideas', but the complicated *thought objects,* which are experienced as wholes but each of which includes more central parts and a *fringe* of vague connections and *feelings* (see *stream of thought*). On this basis James states the psychological law of association (*Principles of Psychology,* vol. I p. 561):

> '*Objects once experienced together tend to become associated in the imagination, so that when any one of them is thought of, the others are likely to be thought of also, in the same order of sequence or coexistence as before.* This statement we may name the law of *mental association by contiguity.* ... Whatever we name the law, since it expresses merely a phenomenon of mental *habit, the most natural way of accounting for it is to conceive it as a result of the laws of habit in the nervous system.*'

By James's descriptions it is made clear how a large part of the human mental activity, not the least the more advanced manifestations of this activity, may be understood as a result of associations. Thus it is through associations that the impressions we receive through sight and hearing promptly in our stream of thought are known as things in our surroundings. Likewise all of the linguistic activity rests on associations. Concerning the difference in the minds of brutes and men James says (vol. II p. 360): '*the most elementary single difference between the human mind and that of brutes lies in this deficiency on the brute's part to associate ideas by similarity*'. Inventors and discoverers are people having a strongly developed ability in *association by similarity*, q.v.

Later philosophers have mostly overlooked James's decisive revision of how to understand associations. They have judged associations from the useless notion of elementary ideas, and thus either have rejected this form of description completely, or have been blind to its power in the description of mental life. Such an attitude is displayed when Gilbert Ryle 60 years after James says (*The Concept of Mind*, p. 303): 'Even the spell-binding, because so promisingly "chemical" principle of the Association of Ideas found its chief practical application in the prompt word-responses voiced aloud by subjects to whom test words were spoken by the experimenter.' Ryle is evidently ignorant of James's revision of the talk of associations and has not understood the central function of associations in mental life.

In behavioristic psychology, which is dominating in the twentieth century, the experience of the stream of thought, and thus the talk of associations, has been put under taboo (see *behaviorism*).

See also *association by similarity, concept, habit, introspection, language, psychology, reasoning, stream of thought.*

Association by similarity: Thus is called *association* between thought objects (see *stream of thought*) that have become connected in the thought merely by having the same abstract property in common, in other words by being similar in some respect. One may for example experience that a lit candle associatively turns the thought to the Moon, by virtue of the light coming from both of them. Association by similarity is part of *reasoning*, q.v., and thus is one of the main ingredients of human genius.

Further references are given in the Literature Appendix.

Astronomy: See *philosophy of science.*

Atom bomb: See *scientific-scholarly activity.*

Attention: The word is used by William James in his *Principles of Psychology* to denote the selection of a part of the thought object for special notice and analysis which is always taking place. See also *perception, stream of thought.* Further references are given in the Literature Appendix.

Augustine: See *word-as-code-of-meaning-fallacy.*

Austin, J. L.: See *knowing, belief.* Further references are given in the Literature Appendix.

Axiom: See *mathematical logic.*

Ayer, Alfred: See *knowing*.

Be, being: See *is*.

Behaviorism: A philosophically inspired attitude to psychology, which arose in the USA around 1910 and which since then has perverted that part of psychology which deals with the relation of people to their non-human surroundings. Behaviorism dictates that the mental life of people is a forbidden subject; that psychology must only concern itself with the observable behaviour of people. As the justification of this attitude is given fallacious, philosophically (Aristotelian) inspired notions of what physicists are doing and what science and scholarship is about.

The idea to wish to talk about common features of human life and activity while refusing to talk of what every person experiences in every waking moment, to wit the *stream of thought*, is so foolish that it is astounding that anyone has pursued it. The name of the psychologist who succeeded in disseminating the folly of behaviorism shall here be left to the oblivion it deserves.

See also *association, introspection, psychology, stream of thought*.

Belief: 'Belief' together with 'knowledge' is among the designations most frequently used by the philosophers who are concerned with people's ways of understanding their surroundings. The philosophical talk of belief suffers from much unclarity, which is related to: (1) the common use of the word 'belief' to designate several different concerns, (2) the addiction of philosophers to logic.

As an example of philosophers' talk about belief we can take the beginning of Lecture XII, Belief, in Bertrand Russell's *The Analysis of Mind:*

'Belief, which is our subject to-day, is the central problem in the analysis of mind. Believing seems the most "mental" thing we do, the thing most remote from what is done by mere matter. The whole intellectual life consists of beliefs, and of the passage from one belief to another by what is called "reasoning". Beliefs give knowledge and error; they are the vehicles of truth and falsehood. Psychology, theory of knowledge and metaphysics revolve about belief, and on the view we take of belief our philosophical outlook largely depends.'

This passage is characteristic of Russell's philosophically presumptuous manner. As the expression of an Aristotelian 'highest truth' Russell pronounces what 'the whole intellectual life consists of'. According to Russell the mind of every person is incessantly passing from one belief to the next, through something he calls reasoning, without in this place or anywhere else in the 308 pages of his book saying anything more about what he understands the word 'reasoning' to say.

Such a passage is embarrassing. If only one had retained the infant's innocence so as to be permitted to say: he has nothing on! The point is, as an account of mental life Russell's presentation is appalling. This must be clear to anyone who gives introspective attention to his or her stream of thought at any waking moment.

The matter does not improve in the continuation of the above quotation, where Russell says:

'Before embarking upon the detailed analysis of belief, we shall do well to note certain requisites which any theory must fulfil.

(1) Just as words are characterized by meaning, so beliefs are characterized by truth or falsehood. And just as meaning consists in relation to the object meant, so truth and falsehood consist in relation to something that lies outside the belief. You may believe that such-and-such a horse will win the Derby. The time comes, and your horse wins or does not win; according to the outcome, your belief was true or false. You may believe that six times nine is fifty-six; in this case also there is a fact which makes your belief false. You may believe that America was discovered in 1492, or that it was discovered in 1066. In one case your belief is true, in the other false; in either case its truth or falsehood depends upon the actions of Columbus, not upon anything present or under your control.'

What is immediately most striking about these examples is the superficiality they display. Russell is committed to the *word-as-code-of-meaning-fallacy,* q.v., and thus takes it for granted that the use of the same word, 'belief', implies that what is talked about in the three examples is one and the same.

Let us look closer at the three examples given by Russell of the kind of belief, and perhaps truth, which in his view forms the basis of the whole of intellectual life.

Example 1 is 'that such-and-such a horse will win the Derby'. But this raises questions, first of all what is implied in saying that a person may, not believe in, but merely attach a meaning to the statement 'that such-and-such a horse will win the Derby'. The answer to this is of course, first of all, that such a person must *be acquainted with* what is being talked about, with the kind of things that usually are meant by 'horse-racing' and 'the Derby'. Thus it should be clear that *mental life, before any belief of the kind Russell talks about comes into the picture, must contain acquaintance with certain aspects of the world* (see *knowing*).

But mere acquaintance with an aspect of the world contains nothing that may be called belief or truth. A person is either acquainted with what is usually called the Derby or is not. If there is to be talk of something that is believed or is known in this connection, it has to be concerned with something additional, something that be may believed or known *about something already known by acquaintance.* Thus it becomes clear why Russell's statement: 'The whole intellectual life consists of beliefs, and of the passage from one belief to another by what is called "reasoning"' is totally impossible as a description of mental life (see also *reasoning*).

That which is believed in Russell's first example is something in the future, a property of the Derby which has been planned to take place. Saying, as Russell does, that the belief that 'such-and-such a horse will win the Derby' is true provided the horse in fact wins, is merely confused talk. As known to anyone who is familiar with the usual locutions, believing about something that is expected to happen in the future is something else than knowing about what has already taken place.

That which is said to be believed in Russell's second example, 'six times nine is fifty-six', is of a different character. The belief is again conditional on acquaintance with certain circumstances of the world, but in this case these circumstances are linguistic habits in a certain society of people, among other things the way the members of this society tend to use such words as 'six', 'times', 'nine', and 'fifty-six'. Unlike most other words, these words in the common understanding are associated with strictly defined notions, the mathematical numbers. Thus it is plausible, though not certain, that the belief the person expresses by the phrase 'six times nine is fifty-six' may be expressed more elaborately in this way: the person believes that the relation which in the common use of language is expressed by the phrase, is mathematically correct. That the belief reasonably may be assumed to be expressible in this way is connected with the form of the phrase, which makes it meaningful to talk about what it expresses mathematically, even though this is not mathematically correct. This is unlike what is the case for phrases of many other forms, e.g. 'six times nine is pumpkin pie'.

Thus the belief Russell talks about in his example 2 is a matter of mathematical correctness. Unlike the Derby, this is not related to the passing of time.

Russell's third example of belief is this: 'You may believe that America was discovered in 1492, or that it was discovered in 1066. In one case your belief is true, in the other false'. In saying so Russell lets us know that the statement 'America was discovered in 1492' is a truth, of the kind that in his view constitutes intellectual life.

These ways of expression are problematic, however. The statement is concerned with something that happened in the year 1492. This year Christopher Columbus with his ship reached the island Cuba and several other islands in the Caribbean Sea, lands that until then had been unknown to Europeans. But these lands were of course well known to their native inhabitants, and the name 'America' was not used for these parts of the world before many years later. Therefore the phrase 'America was discovered' is quite imprecise as a statements of what happened in the year 1492. Moreover, parts of North America had already been visited by the Norse sailor Leif Eriksson around year 1000.

Altogether, Russell's talk of truth in relation to the expression 'America was discovered in 1492' is untenable. The expression is crudely descriptive of certain aspects of the world, of truth there is none (see *description*).

In summary, Russell's presentation in this passage builds on the philosophical view that thoughts consist of statements of belief or truths. The failure of the presentation to stand a closer scrutiny indicates the impossibility of this view (see also *thinking-as-language-fallacy*).

As another approach to understanding belief, Austin and Ryle have examined believing and knowing empirically. They build their investigations upon the common understanding of manners of speaking. This understanding is known introspectively by persons who habitually make use of the manners of speaking in question.

On this ground Austin dismisses the philosophical claim that knowing is a special form of believing. In the article *Other Minds* Austin says:

'There is a singular difference between the two forms of challenge: "*How* do you know?" and "*Why* do you believe?" We seem never to ask "*Why* do you know?" or "*How* do you believe?"'

Ryle finds that both a person's believing something and the person's knowing something, in ordinary talk denotes a personal *habit* or *disposition* of a certain character, in other words a personal tendency to react in certain ways. To believe or to know that the ice is thin is to be disposed to have certain thoughts and to say and do certain things. The difference between believing and knowing is that knowing implies a disposition to succeed in certain matters, while believing does not imply success. For more about this, see *knowing, logic*.

Belief ...

In other contexts the word 'belief' is used in common statements of the form 'A believes in B', where A denotes a person while B may denote anything. Where B denotes a person the expression 'A believes in B' indicates that a certain relation of trust prevails. Where B denotes something other than a person the expression commonly indicates that A feels B as real, see *reality*.

Further references are given in the Literature Appendix.

Bohr, Niels: See *model, paradigm, theory, cause.*

Boole, George: See *mathematical logic.*

Botany: See *philosophy of science.*

Building site: Metaphor for the thought activity, see *stream of thought.*

Calculus: See *mathematical analysis.*

Cause: 'Cause' presents a striking illustration of how manners of speech that are clear and useful in everyday life, when taken over by philosophers give rise to nonsense.

'Cause', Latin causa, has a key position in Aristotle's philosophy, since he maintained that all changes and motions in the things of our surroundings are results of causes. Still earlier Leucippos had declared: 'Nothing happens without a ground but everything through a cause and of necessity.' The explanation of cause in *Dictionary of Philosophy* comes straight from Aristotle and 'cause' enters into the explanation of certain –*isms*.

The talk of causes was taken over by the philosophers of science, such as John Stuart Mill. The confusion in the philosophical talk of causes was laid bare by Bertrand Russell in the article *On the Notion of Cause* from 1912, which is the only antiphilosophical contribution to the literature I have encountered. Here Russell maintains that the talk of causes in scientific contexts is nonsense. He first discusses in detail what is said in a philosophical dictionary about causes, and demonstrates how it is unclear and self-contradictory. He then describes what is talked about in advanced science, taking as his example the astronomers' theory of the motion of the Moon. Here the astronomers do not talk of causes at all. The Moon theory combines the results of the astronomers' numerous measurements of the position of the Moon in the sky with that differential equation which according Newtonian mechanics describes the motion of the Moon under the influence of the Earth, the Sun, and the other planets. As a result the astronomers develop a mathematical formula, which makes it possible to compute the position of the Moon in the sky at any desired moment. It turns out that the position computed from this formula agrees within a quite small tolerance with the positions that have been measured. Thus the astronomers have developed a good *description* of the motion of the Moon.

In spite of his analysis, which concluded that the word cause is useless in science, Russell in his later works continued to talk unclearly about causes, thus at many places in *The Analysis of Mind* (see for example quotation under *perception*). Also physicists, for example Niels Bohr, have continued to talk unclearly as though physics were concerned with causes.

What the philosophers, including Russell, entirely overlook is the meaningful talk of causes, such as it is common in everyday life. For example one may during a walk have occasion to ask one's companion: Why are you limping, what is the cause of your limp? Then the answer may be: Because I have a stone in my shoe. The context here is that in our question we have understood a comparison of two situations that are alike in all but a few respects. We have compared our companion's present limping with the same person's non-limping manner of walking at other occasions. Now we inquire into other circumstances that make the two situations different. Thus causes enter into a special *form of description* of the present situation. This form is the domain of the service technician: Why does the car make a rattling sound, what is the cause?

The philosophical nonsense about causes arises when it is claimed that every change has a cause, for example if you ask about the cause that I sit here and press the keys of the computer. This question has no meaningful answer. My reaction to it would be: what else should I be doing?

See also *mathematical logic*. Further references are given in the Literature Appendix.

Ceres: See *philosophy of science.*

Chargaff, Erwin: See *scientific-scholarly activity.*

Chomsky, Noam: See *language-rule-fallacy, word-as-code-of-meaning-fallacy.*

Classical mechanics: See *Newtonian mechanics.*

Collin, Finn: See *language-as-something-fallacy, mathematical logic, reality.*

Concept: Unclear talk about 'concepts' and 'conception' lies at the bottom of much philosophical nonsense, with close relation to the philosophical *language-fallacies*. By this nonsense the understanding of the basic role of concepts in human mental life is confounded.

In everyday life the word concept is met for example in the game called Twenty Questions. The game is that the participants in turn try to discover a word, merely from the answers yes or no to at most twenty questions about what the word designates. Normally each round of the game starts by the questioner being told whether the word to be found designates something from the realm of animals, the realm of plants, the realm of minerals, or else a concept. Thus concepts are understood negatively. According to this way of speaking concepts are things designated by words that *do not* designate something from the realms of animals, plants, and minerals. Whether at closer look it makes sense to speak of concepts in this way, normally is asked by no one in the game.

People also talk about concepts in scientific contexts. Thus Einstein in a passage quoted in the article about *foundations* says: 'The scientific way of forming concepts differs from that which we use in our daily life, not basically, but merely in the more precise definition of concepts and conclusions.' This statement is problematic, partly by the assumption that concepts are known things, partly by claiming that in daily life we form them, and then by talking about definition of concepts.

That which Einstein hints at in his statement presumably may be illustrated by the following example concerning heat phenomena. In daily life, and long before the rise of modern physics, people have known that things may be cold and warm and that they may change from one to the other. In ordinary conversations, in certain situations and contexts, clear meaning has been associated with such statements as: the pot was so hot that I burnt my fingers on it; it is not cold enough to go skating; the icy cold was over the land for several weeks.

But to a physicist these locutions are insufficient. The physicists seek ways of talking in more detail and more precisely about heat phenomena, and in this endeavor have found it convenient to talk about, among other things, temperature, specific heat, heat of melting, and heat of vaporization. These are designations of measurable quantities that are descriptive of properties of the things in our surroundings and that have a certain connection with what in ordinary conversations is associated with the talk of cold and warm. The quantities may be measured with the aid of devices, such as thermometers, constructed in special ways invented by the physicists.

In the light of this example it may be seen that Einstein's talk of concepts is misleading. That which we make use of, in daily life as well as in scientific description, are not concepts but *descriptive designations*, as for example 'warm', 'cold', 'temperature'. That which is defined more precisely in scientific work is not concepts, but what in certain contexts is to be understood by statements in which selected descriptive designations are used in certain ways. Speaking of concepts in this context confuses the understanding of an important aspect of mental life that will be discussed below.

As illustration of similar philosophical misconceptions around concepts we may take for example *Indledning* to Hartnack's *Filosofiske essays*. Hartnack's concern about concepts, whatever they are, is clear enough when, on page 11, he writes:

'... it holds for all philosophical arguments that they concern the logic of concepts. In order to study the logic of a concept one studies the sentences and expressions in which the words in question enter. One studies the concept "gladness" by studying such sentences as "He is glad", and "I am glad".'

But by using the phrase 'the words in question', which does not designate anything definite in the context, even this concluding program declaration indicates the unclarity in Hartnack's talk about concepts.

The unclarity is displayed in more detail in the previous pages of Hartnack's book. Here he has first talked about, among other things, 'what the word "cause" means' and about 'the logical rules for the use of a word'. He has then said that it 'suits the purpose better to talk about the logic of a concept' and has followed this up with this explanation:

'We may, if we do not read too much into it, say that the concept "gladness" is what is common to the following three sentences (1) "They were all glad", (2) "There was much gladness", (3) "It inspired gladness".'

With this a dense mist has descended over the scene. We have first been told not to read too much into it. This means that Hartnack explains 'concept', the core of what he calls philosophy, in terms of an explanation that he is not willing to defend! Then, in Aristotelian fashion, 'concept' is defined by what it *is* (q.v.). Which, says Hartnack, is what is common to the three sentences. To which I have to say, this is totally unclear to me.

Why is it unclear? Because the sentences have infinitely many things in common. To mention only a few of their common properties: the sentences all have a capital first letter; they are all expressed in a certain English style, having English verbs in the past tense; they are printed on paper; they appear together in a certain printed form here on my desk; they have fewer than five words; they have fewer than six words; etc. etc. *ad infinitum*.

To this Hartnack will perhaps say that I act the fool, since obviously what he is thinking of is something that is common to what the sentences mean. To this I will answer that what a linguistic utterance means depends entirely upon the context in which it uttered. As given by Hartnack, divorced from any context, the sentences mean nothing definite. Thus (1) talks about 'They', without designating anybody, (2) talks about 'There was' without any explanation about where or when, and (3) talks about 'It' without any indication of what it is.

In reply to this Hartnack may perhaps say that ordinary people will say without any hesitation that they understand what the sentences mean. To this I will answer that what ordinary people mean when they say they understand words and sentences divorced from a context, at closer look says nothing about that the words and sentences in question should have a meaning independently of a context. When a philosopher presents a sentence for consideration, this presentation is in itself a context. The meaning of a sentence to a person in this context depends on that the person is able to *imagine a situation in a certain society in which the sentence in ordinary conversation might means something definite.* Pronouncements about the meaning of sentences in the kind of context in which Hartnack presents them is implicitly understood to be concerned with the *linguistic habits* of people of a certain society.

To this may be added that this way of determining what sentences mean delimits no definite boundary. It opens for admitting that *any signal whatever may be said to mean anything,* simply by admitting any context, including games, use of special codes, etc.

In this perspective it is clear enough what is in a word, for example 'gladness'. What we mean when we say that 'gladness' is a word is that it enters into the linguistic habits of a certain circle of people, i.e. habits that associate words with thought objects. As a matter of fact, a large number of the persons who nowadays inhabit the British Isles and North America habitually use the spoken or written word 'gladness' in certain forms of *descriptions of the moods of persons.* These habits are well known among these persons. If one wants to describe these habits more closely one may obtain information about them by talking with the persons and by reading what they write, in the way scholars of linguistics proceed when they investigate linguistic habits. The results of such investigations have already been collected in dictionaries, which are catalogs of linguistic habits in certain societies.

But with this talk about linguistic habits nothing has been said about concepts. Hartnack's approach is a blind alley, the *concept-is-word-fallacy,* where one arrives when one tries to describe concepts starting from something linguistic, from certain words. This approach to the matter is grounded in the *word-as-code-of-meaning-* and the *language-as-something-fallacies,* qq.v.

The impassable access to concepts through words is the more unfortunate thereby that it blocks the way to a real understanding of the important aspect of mental life that concepts are. But as a source of such understanding one has to avoid the philosophers and instead seek classical psychology, William James's *Principles of Psychology.* *Conception* is used by James to designate the *mental function* of distinguishing and retaining a distinct and permanent *subject of discourse* in the stream of thought. Through this mental function an item with which the person is *acquainted* may be *retained in the person's stream of thought* in the form of a concept (see *knowing, stream of thought*). The person will subsequently in his or her stream of thought be able to recall the concept, which retains an *unchangeable identity* to the thought.

Concept ...

As stressed by James, this unchangeability holds for the concept as it is recalled in the stream of thought, but not necessarily for what the concept knows. James calls this sense of sameness (the principle of constancy of the mind's meanings) the very keel and backbone of human thinking.

That which we may retain as a concept in our stream of thought may be of widely different kinds and characters. We may, as said by James, 'conceive realities supposed to be extra-mental, as steam-engine; fictions, as mermaid; or mere *entia rationis,* like difference or nonentity.'

Conception and use of the corresponding concepts happen all the time in all people. All the impressions we receive through sight and hearing about our surroundings promptly call up in our stream of thought, by habitual associations, the constant concepts of the things we know.

All the time we form new concepts. Many of our organized activities, for example, are associated with concepts. Perhaps I decide on a certain day to make a shopping round during the day. The moment I make this decision I have formed a concept, which in my thought need not be tied to any designation, but which I might, for example, denote 'my shopping trip 1998 March 31'. In the time before the trip itself I may then in my thought return to 'my shopping trip 1998 March 31', and perhaps add details about where it shall be going and what shall be done on the way. But during these further considerations the concept 'my shopping trip 1998 March 31' remains unchanged in my thought, as the stable anchor of the details in my thought.

Concepts and conception as described by James are properties of the stream of thought we experience each of us. As such concepts have no special relation to words or phrases, but they may, like any other object in the stream of thought, be associated with words.

But concepts are personal. It makes no sense to ask whether my concept of something is the same as yours. A philosopher may concern himself with his own personal concepts and their logic, but in doing so he says nothing about my concepts, most of which have nothing to do with logic. Talking about concepts that are not tied to a personal stream of thought is nonsense.

See also *perception, psychology, thinking-as-language-fallacy.*

Concept-is-word-fallacy: This is the notion that concepts are tied to words, and that each concept thereby, through the *word-as-code-of-meaning-fallacy*, may be assigned a meaning which is independent of individual persons. The fallacy is expressed, for example, in the title given by Ryle to a book, The Concept of Mind. By here talking about 'The Concept', in definite form, it is implied that what the book is about may be something which is common to an indefinite community of persons. The concept-is-word-fallacy reflects a defective understanding of what in William James's words is the keel and backbone of human thinking: *concepts,* q.v.

See also *logic.*

Conception: See *concept.*

Consciousness: The word consciousness, together with some others similar to it, illustrates the confusion arising from the Aristotelian talk of what something *is* or whether it *exists*, qq.v.

The nonsense around 'consciousness' derives from several common locutions. Thus we may say that a person has *lost consciousness*, *is unconscious*, or has *regained consciousness*. With these locutions we describe certain aspects of our *stream of thought* (q.v.), aspects that every person usually experiences every day, among other things as the difference between being asleep and awake.

By other locutions we may in certain situations say that we *are* or *make ourselves conscious* about something we are doing. These locutions relate to the fact that a large part of what we do in daily life happens according to well trained habits, in such a way that a series of actions follow each other in a smooth sequence, which may take place without the need for us to pay much attention to each action of the sequence. Instead our attention may be directed at some other activity. But while this other activity is in progress the actions of the habitual sequence remain in the *fringe* of the thought object of the activity, and we may at any time turn our attention away from the activity, toward the actions of the habitual sequence. During a meal conversation we may, for example, turn the attention away from what we are talking about, toward the movement of a cup we are doing with our hand. In ordinary conversations we may describe this by saying that we become or make ourselves conscious of what we are in the middle of doing.

But out of these ordinary, descriptive locutions develop, by a philosophical twist, quite different locutions, that refer to our stream of consciousness as a something, 'the consciousness', which is located in a definite place, a kind of theatre stage. The stream of thought is described as a performance enacted upon an internal stage, which is watched by an internal eye. That which we experience at a certain moment is said to be 'in the consciousness'. Other things going on within us are said to take place 'unconsciously'. Further it is said that certain influences upon what is 'in the consciousness' may originate from a place that is unknown to us, 'the subconsciousness'. All this gives rise to endless philosophical squabbles about whether consciousness and subconsciousness *exist* (see *existence*) and where they are located.

The controversy over the 'existence' of 'the unconscious' or 'subconsciousness' is in part directed at what is happening in creative activity. Thus the mathematician Poincaré has described his work process, and has noted his experience that the solution of a mathematical problem sometimes appears to him suddenly and unexpectedly, entirely out of context with the situation in which he has found himself, after a period of several days without thoughts to the problem in question. He maintains that such experience shows that during the previous days an 'unconscious thought process' has been in progress, and thus *proves* that 'the unconscious' exists. For more about this, consult the Literature Appendix.

The controversies around these locutions illustrate the confusion arising from the philosophical talk about existence. If we are to achieve clarity we have, first of all, to find out *what the words we use designate,* if anything. Thus if we are to make sense of the talk about 'the unconscious' or 'subconsciousness', the first condition is to make clear what 'the conscious' and 'consciousness' designate. But this is where the explanation fails, since 'consciousness' does not designate anything clearly.

The core of the matter is the *stream of thought* (q.v.) experienced by everyone of us in each of our waking moments, and in particular the way new and sometimes unexpected thought objects appear in it.

If one says that the usual stream of thought is a conscious activity it is overlooked that the stream of thought is changing all the time and quite ordinarily contains objects that are new in the context, in the sense that they have not been present in the fringe of the current object. Such new objects appear to most of us innumerable times in daily life. Perhaps we have, according to our habit, gone to the kitchen about the time we usually have a meal. But where do we begin the preparations? There are several possibilities, what do we want to eat, and what do we do first? Perhaps we find that the store is empty of bread, what do we do now? Perhaps it now occurs to us, as a new thought, that we may postpone the meal and start by doing a round of shopping. Or that we may do with biscuits and just make a note of bread on the shopping list. Etc. etc. In such situations we will presumably always hesitate for a shorter or longer time, while *waiting for the new idea to appear* in the stream of thought.

Similar hesitations occur in ordinary conversation. That which we do in fact say comes to us at the very moment of speaking, after the hesitation that always precedes an utterance. Even if one in a special situation has to prepare what to say carefully, one will find that what comes out in fact is something else, perhaps with the same meaning, but still different. Thus we are throughout life countless times faced with having to find out what we are now going to do.

But how do these notions about what we may do come forth? How does it occur to us that we may go shopping instead of preparing food? One answer is to say that we have *experience* helping us to see possible solutions of the current problem. By other locutions we have *habits* such that a certain combination of circumstances in which we find ourselves, in a certain situation, releases the image of something we may do. No matter what words we use for the description, it is an everyday experience that what comes forth in our stream of thought in this kind of situation is something that has *not* been present in the *fringe* of the current *thought object,* but is new in the context. And thus in terms of the locutions that start from 'consciousness' as a place having a certain contents, it would have to be designated as something coming from somewhere else, from 'the unconscious'.

But the talk of 'consciousness' and 'the unconscious' in this context is misleading. These phrases imply that thoughts are kinds of elements, that may be found in various locations and move around between them, rather like pictures and documents. But such a description of the stream of thought is entirely misleading. That which is found in the stream of thought at a certain moment is an enormously complicated whole, which cannot be divided into elements or ideas. The thought of going shopping instead of preparing food is not an isolated element, but a kind of modification of or addition to the thought object we experience in the situation. This thought object already in its fringe has a wealth of feelings and images, like any other thought object. It may without further ado accommodate an additional possibility.

In this way the stream of thought in its ordinary development incessantly comes to hold something new, something that was not in the fringe of current thought object, something that has not been there to be found merely by a redirection of the attention. But the new that comes in is not accidental. It is something that is tied by *association* to the current thought object. Thus it depends on the *habits,* the *dispositions,* we have acquired in our previous life.

But our habits are not things that come forth in our stream of thought, something we might be said to be conscious of. This is not because they live in 'subconsciousness' or are 'unconscious', but because habits are not things of such a kind that they *might* appear in the stream of thought. The person who has the habit of smoking cigarettes does not experience the habit as such. What is experienced is that the urge to smoke suddenly comes forth.

In the perspective of this description of the stream of thought and its continual development it becomes clear that the talk of 'the unconscious' or 'subconsciousness', as something that should take place in the same way as the (conscious) stream of thought every one of us experiences, but which should be hidden from us, is merely misleading. Our experience may be described effortlessly in terms of the *stream of thought*, the *thought objects* with their *fringes* and their habitual *associations*.

In other words, what is said here about consciousness revolves around the *choice of description forms* for mental life. What is wrong with 'consciousness' and 'subconsciousness' is that descriptions in terms of these designations get into a muddle.

See also *thought-as-perception-mistake*.

Crick, Francis: See *DNA, foundations, scientific-scholarly activity, Watson.*

Definition: Denotes a technique of description. Through a definition a descriptive element, most often a designation, is joined to those that are already understood or have been introduced in the context of the description.

Descartes, René: Descartes is one of the big guns in philosophy. His essay *Discours sur la Methode* (Discourse on Method) is read as a classic by every French child, and the climax of the text: *Je pense, donc je suis* (I think, so I am), has become a philosophical slogan.

And so, what do we find in this essay? It starts like this:

'Good sense is, of all things among men, the most equally distributed; for every one thinks himself so abundantly provided with it, that those even who are the most difficult to satisfy in everything else, do not usually desire a larger measure of this quality than they already possess.'

What can one, as reader, make of this? Is it to be taken as a joke? As the introduction to a serious contribution one may be permitted to look at it more closely. Take the very first sentence. It looks like an argument, but what is the point? It says that good sense must be equally distributed among men. But what is the sense of this? Is good sense a sort of cake which may be distributed? What nonsense! And the ground for this claim is stated to be, that nobody complains about having received too little. By the same argument both poverty and toothache must be equally distributed among men. How foolish! Upon this start I, as reader, must have a deep distrust in Descartes's ability to find adequate expression for psychological matters.

Descartes proceeds to tell about his studies in Paris and his travelling life, with the constant burden that he was set upon distinguishing between the true and the false. With his presumptuous urge to possess the truth he was a true philosopher in Aristotle's footsteps. On his way towards this goal he formulates his program, to doubt anything that is not certainly true. In this way he finally arrives at something he can use, something he thinks is true: *je pense,* I think.

And immediately logic goes into action, he may draw a logical conclusion (hurrah!): *je pense, donc je suis: I think, hence I am.* From this Descartes proceeds to derive that his 'I', the 'I' that *is* (q.v.), is 'a substance whose whole essence or nature consists only in thinking, and which, that it may exist, has need of no place, nor is dependent on any material thing'. And so his argumentation continues, he proves that there is a perfect being, God, etc. etc.

All this builds upon poor observation and misleading manners of speaking. Take the initial: 'I think'. This according to Descartes is an adequate expression of what happens during his pondering over all sorts of errors, and thus what, in view of this activity, is the evidence that an 'I' is there. But the words 'I think' is a misleading expression of our experience as human beings. As stressed by William James the primary, elementary experience should be expressed by: *thinking goes on* (see *thought-as-perception-mistake*). Our *stream of thought* (q.v.) is not the result of something we are doing. The stream of thought goes on whether we want it or not, as experienced by thousands of people, who in long sleepless hours have no greater desire than to have the stream of thought cease. But they cannot make it.

As described by James our feeling of being an 'I', separated from other people, comes not from an experience of actively producing the stream of thought, but as a *property of the stream of thought,* as we have experienced it during our life. An object in our stream of thought may be *acquainted with other thought objects* in the same stream of thought, and *feel that they all belong together as ours.* This feeling of our I is an immediate experience, which cannot be supported by any kind of logic.

The second part of Descartes's slogan, 'hence I am', is no better than 'I think'. Even if we would accept that the thinking establishes an 'I', there is no sense in 'hence I am'. 'I am' is no statement, it is an incomplete fragment of a sentence. In ordinary conversational context one may say, e.g. 'I am sleepy', 'I am busy', 'I am a mechanic'. But 'I am' without further specification is nonsense. Only philosophers, the followers of Aristotle, concern themselves with such (see *is*). They may understand it in any way they like, and quarrel about it. This they have now been doing for several thousand years.

Descartes's continued argumentation is similarly defective. His statement 'I think' may be taken as an expression of his introspective observation of a property of himself. Even though his formulation 'I think' is misleading, he describes something he experiences, to wit *the stream of thought*. Descartes now continues:

> 'In the next place, I attentively examined what I was, and as I observed that I could suppose that I had no body, and that there was no world nor any place in which I might be.'

This unclear statement is, like 'I think', an expression of superficial introspection. The unclarity lies in the phrase 'I could suppose'. With the ordinary understanding of the words one may suppose anything; what one supposes says nothing about the way of the world. But in Descartes's way of speaking, what he says he supposes is very much a matter of the world. And what he says is blatantly wrong. As every one of us may ascertain, every one of our thoughts, irrespective of where it is otherwise directed, includes more or less definite feelings of our body and of our present position in space and time. As I sit at this moment with my thoughts directed towards these formulations of my critique of Descartes, I have at all times feelings of all parts of my body, faint pressures, aches, itches, and in addition I can at no moment avoid feeling my presence in my usual room, a morning with the winter sunshine coming in through the window. Such feelings are part of every thought object; they are to be found at any time in what William James calls their *fringe*.

Descartes's saying that his thinking might be what it is independently of his body and his presence in time and space is directly contradicted by the account he has just given of his life. The 'I' he experiences is precisely that carnal person who over a number of years has spoken to many people in several countries and among other things been soldier in Germany.

Thus Descartes is the typical poor observer. He is so keen at finding confirmations of his *logic* that he is blind to what is present in his stream of thought in all his wake moments.

The influence of the *feelings* in the fringes of our thought objects upon our understanding is confirmed explicitly by Descartes himself. Thus one page after the places quoted above he writes:

'And as I observed that in the words *I think, hence I am*, there is nothing at all which gives me assurance of their truth beyond this, that I see very clearly that in order to think it is necessary to exist, I concluded that I might take, as a general rule, the principle, that all the things which we very clearly and distinctly conceive are true.'

The issue is what in this context lies in the words 'I see very clearly'. The word 'see' here obviously has to be understood, not literally denoting something Descartes perceives by his eyes, but as a metaphor, since what he sees: 'that in order to think it is necessary to exist', is not visible to the eyes. That which Descartes describes by his expression can only be understood as a *feeling* accompanying that which he experiences at the phrase 'in order to think it is necessary to exist'. In other words, Descartes's finding that 'this is true' builds upon an immediate feeling, which accompanies his experience of the phrase. Thus Descartes, as far as he is concerned, confirms the description of reality given by William James, see *reality*.

But Descartes's argumentation gives him this result:

'I hence concluded that I was a substance whose whole essence or nature consists only in thinking, and which, that it may exist, has need of no place, nor is dependent on any material thing; so that "I", that is to say, the mind by which I am what I am, is wholly distinct from the body.'

This talk about his 'I', that which *is,* being 'a substance whose whole essence or nature consists only in thinking', is directly in the Aristotelian philosophical tradition, see *essence*.

Descartes's result was accepted by generations of later philosophers, but has given rise to endless philosophical headaches. Descartes's discussion was rejected in 1890 by William James in his *Principles of Psychology*. James is not concerned with truth, but with description. As he stresses, a description of mental life that sees the stream of thought as a panorama observed by an internal eye, in the way the world around us is observed by our real eyes, leads to all sorts of paradoxes, see *consciousness, thought-as-perception-mistake*.

Ryle takes up the same theme 60 years later, without acquaintance with James's classical work, in his book *The Concept of Mind,* under the label 'The ghost in the machine'.

See also *artificial intelligence, psychology.*

Description: Philosophers do not concern themselves with description; they are superior to such useful undertaking. A philosopher on a visit to a town is not interested in a description of it, he is only interested in finding the *essence* of the town, that which makes it what it *is.* In order to find his way in the streets the philosopher must have slaves, as Aristotle had them in the Greek society. They may then use descriptions of the town, for example a street map.

In description we give *explicit expression to properties* of something with which we are acquainted. This expression may be verbal, that is it may consist of something we pronounce, or it may be written text, or it may be anything else, drawn figures, programs in a computer, models of any kind.

But anything in the world has infinitely many properties (see *property*). By contrast, every description is finite, consisting, for example, of a certain number of words or a certain number of parts of a model. Thus the description may only give expression to a part of the properties of what it describes. And thus no description is correct or true of what it describes, in any logical sense. Each and every description is incomplete.

The value of a description is that a person who understands it may use it in *reasoning*, q.v.

The understanding of a description is dependent upon it being perceived by a person in a certain context, similarly as any linguistic expression. That which is described must be known by acquaintance by the person, see *knowing*.

Every description is grounded in a *choice of elements and forms of expression,* the *description form* for short, in which the description is expressed. Thus structure and other formal properties belong, not to what is described, but to the description form.

To philosophers the idea of description is so remote that they will sometimes engage themselves in a major project of description without themselves noticing it. This we find in Gilbert Ryle's *The Concept of Mind.* By Ryle's own declaration, the main purpose of his book is to discuss and explode what he calls the official doctrine about the nature and place of minds. Ryle says on p. 13:

> 'The official doctrine, which hails chiefly from Descartes, is something like this. With the doubtful exceptions of idiots and infants in arms every human being has both a body and a mind. Some would prefer to say that every human being is both a body and a mind. His body and his mind are ordinarily harnessed together, but after the death of the body his mind may continue to exist and function.'

Ryle continues to identify this as the doctrine of 'the ghost in the machine'.

In the view of the present discussion, this explanation is in need of clarification. The critical issue is the meaning of 'is' (or 'has') in 'every human is (has) both a body and a mind', 'is' being the most ambiguous word of the language. What will be claimed is that to make sense of Ryle's whole discussion throughout his book, 'is' ('has') in this context has to be understood as an abbreviation of something like *may from a certain point of view be described as (having)*. This is in contrast to other uses of 'is', for example in 'The critical issue is the meaning ...', where 'is' stands for 'may be identified as', or in 'This is in contrast ...', where 'is' stands for 'displays itself'.

In other words, the present claim is that the whole of Ryle's discussion may properly be regarded as a question of the *proper or coherent manner of describing human beings*. In support of this claim it may be noted that in many places of the book Ryle himself talks of description, see *logic*.

As discussed under *scientific-scholarly activity*, description may reasonably be claimed to be the core of science. More specifically, the scientific-scholarly activity is a matter of *coherent description*. For more of this, consult the Literature Appendix.

See also *belief, cause, knowledge, language of science, law of nature, model, perception, spiritism, theory*.

Description form: Any description consists of certain elements, such as words, tables, curves, or others, combined in a certain way.

In working out a description, the *choice of description form* is decisive. This choice is by no means given by the aspect of the world the description aims at describing. On the contrary, in the development of scientific descriptions it has time after time been found that the choice of a new form of description of some aspect of the world has been a crucial step. A good example is Niels Bohr's epoch making new description of the hydrogen atom from 1913. Up till 1913 the physicists described the hydrogen atom as an electron moving in a closed orbit around a proton, like a planet around the Sun. In Bohr's description there is no mention that the electron is at any place, or that it moves. Bohr says merely that the atom as a whole, that is electron plus proton, may find itself in various stationary states of different energies, and that the atom as a whole may jump from one state to another, while also absorbing or emitting a quantum of light having its energy equal to the difference of energy of the two states. This description form was found in the following years to be immensely fruitful for describing the energy states and light emission of all kinds of atoms.

As another striking example of the dependence of a scientific discovery upon description form may be mentioned Watson and Crick's determination of the structure of DNA with the aid of mechanical molecular models, see *scientific-scholarly activity*.

See also *cause, language of science, paradigm*. Further references are given in the Literature Appendix.

Determinism: The philosophical talk about determinism and determined events builds chiefly upon *Newtonian mechanics* and its success. Newtonian mechanics deals with how things move among themselves. There is talk merely about the masses and mutual positions in space of things. Any other properties of things, what they consist of, their hardness, colors, how they react with another, their way of behaving upon heating or cooling, and many other things, all this has no place in Newtonian mechanics.

But as soon as Newton had presented his description the philosophers took over. Their argumentation in rough outline was this: In Newton's description we have what we have looked for for millennia: the highest truth about the world. All what happens in the world is nothing more than matter in motion, and motion happens as described in Newton's equation.

Determinism ...

But from the form of this equation it follows, that provided we know the positions and velocities of every particle of matter in the world at one definite moment, we will be able to compute the positions and velocities of everything in the world at any later moment. It follows that the universe is a machine that moves along, mercilessly, blindly. This is the notion denoted *determinism*.

But this notion does not stand up to even a superficial examination. It presupposes that Newton's mechanical description fits completely with what happens in the world as we know it. This finds no support, neither in what *has* been found nor in what *might* be found. Take for example the tides. This is well known from daily life along all coasts of the oceans. Newton showed that the rough features of the tides, namely the daily and monthly periods of its changes, could be described in terms of the gravitational influence from the Sun and Moon upon the rotating Earth. But Newton's description was quite crude. It only accounted for the overall features of the phenomenon. In the face of the countless manifestations of the tides, its interplay with winds, weather, and geographical conditions, Newton's description is powerless. It is entirely impossible to get a usable answer to the question whether all these phenomena may be described as matter in motion according to Newton's equation. The claim that the motions we see happening before our eyes agree with Newton's equation can never be verified.

What is said here about Newtonian mechanics holds quite similarly for the more recent descriptions of physics, such as quantum mechanics.

And so the talk about determinism, the claim that the world can be understood as a machine, is a groundless philosophical postulate, without support in the descriptions of physics.

See also *–ism*.

Disposition: The word is used here about persons' habits of thought and feeling, as by Ryle. In particular, a person's linguistic ability is understood as the collection of that person's dispositions to associate words and other linguistic elements with thought objects. See also *belief, habit, knowing, knowledge, language, logic*.

DNA: See *Crick, scientific-scholarly activity, Watson*.

Durant, Will: See *truth*.

Eddington, Arthur Stanley: Eddington was one of the most important astrophysicists of his generation. His main field of interest was the internal constitution of the stars, which he described in terms of the, at that time, novel theory of the atom. He also contributed to the mathematical formulation of Einstein's general theory of relativity. In *The Nature of the Physical World* he has posed himself the task to present what he calls the philosophical results of the great changes in scientific thinking up to 1927. See *Popper, psychology, reality, thinking-as-language-fallacy, truth*.

Einstein, Albert: Einstein is a prominent example of a scientist with an awe-inspired/naïve relation to the sayings of the philosophers. In Einstein's philosophically oriented statements one finds a peculiar mixture of significant insight (see *foundations, science*) and superficial fallacy (see *concept, language of science, word-as-code-of-meaning-fallacy*).

Electrical charge: See *reality*.

Epistemological relativism: Defined in *Dictionary of Philosophy* as the theory that all human knowledge is relative to the knowing mind and to the conditions of the body and sense organs. The explanation is unclear by its talk about 'knowledge', as a noun. See also *–ism, knowing, knowledge.*

Essence: A large part of the philosophical nonsense, including the philosophers' explanations of certain *–isms*, is grounded in the talk of essence. It goes back to Aristotle's talk about form. In *Dictionary of Philosophy* we get the following scholastic 'explanation': The essence of a thing is its nature considered independently of its existence. We are then told that this essence strictly speaking is only known in one case: man is a rational animal. This is the kind of nonsense which is repeated *ad nauseam* in the literary review literature. See also *existence, is.*

The essence nonsense may be found in full flower in a passage in chapter XV, *Science and Mysticism*, in Eddington's *The Nature of the Physical World,* see *truth.*

The philosophical nonsense about essence was laid bare by William James in a passage of his account of *reasoning.* This passage may serve as an example of James's lively and direct style (*Principles of Psychology,* vol. II p. 332-334):

> 'When we conceive of S merely as M (of vermilion merely as a mercury-compound, for example), we neglect all the other attributes which it may have, and attend exclusively to this one. We mutilate the fulness of S's reality. Every reality has an infinity of aspects or properties. ... Vermilion is not only a mercury-compound, it is vividly red, heavy, and expensive, it comes from China, and so on, *in infinitum.* ... All ways of conceiving a concrete fact, if they are true ways at all, are equally true ways. *There is no property* ABSOLUTELY *essential to any one thing.* The same property which figures as the essence of a thing on one occasion becomes a very inessential feature upon another. Now that I am writing, it is essential that I conceive my paper as a surface for inscription. If I failed to do that, I should have to stop my work. But if I wished to light a fire, and no other materials were by, the essential way of conceiving the paper would be as combustible material; and I need then have no thought of any of its other destinations. It is really *all* that it is: a combustible, a writing surface, a thin thing, a hydrocarbonaceous thing, a thing eight inches one way and ten another, a thing just one furlong east of a certain stone in my neighbor's field, an American thing, etc., etc., *ad infinitum.* Whichever one of these aspects of its being I temporarily class it under, makes me unjust to the other aspects. But as I always am classing it under one aspect or another, I am always unjust, always partial, always exclusive. My excuse is necessity—the necessity which my finite and practical nature lays upon me. My thinking is first and last and always for the sake of my doing, and I can only do one thing at a time. ...
>
> Men are so ingrainedly partial that, for common-sense and scholasticism (which is only common-sense grown articulate), the notion that there is no one quality genuinely, absolutely, and exclusively essential to anything is almost unthinkable. ...'

See also *knowing, nonsense, rationality, reality, thinking-as-language-fallacy.*

Exist: See *existence.*

Existence: Together with 'exist' the word belongs to the handful that philosophers are forever using; it appears in their explanation of several *–isms*, q.v.

So once again we find the Danish philosopher Zinkernagel worried about existence in pronouncements quoted in the newspaper Weekendavisen for 1997 Dec. 23. With all their solemnity, these pronouncements upon simple considerations prove themselves to be unclear and incoherent.

Take first what supposedly was the main question in Zinkernagel's Thesis: Does the world around us exist? According to statements from Søren Kjørup and Finn Collin in the same newspaper the question should be understood in connection with what they call 'the basic rules of language' and 'the logic of daily language'.

But merely a bit of ordinary reflection is sufficient to establish that as expression of daily language the question 'Does the world around us exist?' is unclear, foggy. Anyone knows that what is ordinarily expressed when one asks whether something exists, depends entirely on the character of that 'something'. Sometimes one may ask whether a certain, named person still exists. In such cases we want to know whether the person is still alive or is dead. In other cases one may ask whether a certain, particular thing exists. One might, for example, ask whether Haydn's manuscript score of the symphony with the title Le Midi still exists. In yet other cases we may ask about the existence of an enterprise of a certain character; one may, for example, ask whether the restaurant La Petite Hostellerie in Rue de la Harpe in Paris still exists.

One thing which is common to these locutions is that the item whose existence is being queried has limited permanence. Both the person, the score, and the restaurant, have come into being at a definite time, and during a certain period after that time they are understood to retain an identity of a certain character, even though they also are subject to changes, for example by ageing. What we get to know through the answer to the question whether they (still) exist, is, among other things, whether there is still a possibility of getting into contact with them.

But there are many things in daily life of which we cannot reasonably ask whether they exist. Perhaps I hear a bang coming from the street outside. It comes and goes, but who would ask whether it exists? Or I see a spot of light on my bookshelf, sunshine coming through the window. The spot changes, it comes and goes, but what clear meaning would it have to talk about that it is the same from one minute to the next, or that it exists? Or cows. A certain cow exists for a certain period of time, but cows in general, what meaning could it have to say, either that they exist or that they do not? Neither a bang, nor a spot of light, nor cows, are things one might have occasion to get into contact with. Thus there are many things in the world of which there is usually no talk whether they exist. Both the question and any answer to it would be unclear.

The world around us, that the philosophers like to talk about, is something which cannot sensibly be said to exist. The word 'world' is sometimes used in ordinary talking to denote something that lies outside an already specified, intimate environment, usually of people. This intimate environment may embrace a single person, or a few persons. One may say that a loving couple is lost to the world.

But the philosophers' talk of a world without further specification is merely obscure. Thus the question whether the world exists is unclear and not worth attention. But the philosophers insist on, not only posing the question, but on getting a sharp answer, yes or no. This they have been quarrelling about since Aristotle, and for all one can tell will continue doing so also for the coming two thousand years.

See also *language-rule-fallacy, logic, reality.*

Explanation: In scientific contexts an explanation is an account of a phenomenon that builds upon regarding the phenomenon as a particular case of a class of similar phenomena, that class having been *described* scientifically. For example an explanation that a stone released from a certain height falls to the ground is that all heavy bodies behave in this way.

Fact: The word fact is encountered at central spots of the writings of philosophers and enters into the philosophers' explanations of certain *–isms.*

Ordinarily we talk about facts in the context of specific events, for example such that have given rise to legal issues. Facts are descriptions of past events, typically of where certain persons have been present at certain times and what they have been doing, e.g. 'X was riding his bicycle at 23.05 p.m. on October 3 in Bredgade, without a headlight'. Such facts form the basis for applying the rules of the criminal law about guilt and punishment.

Philosophers also talk about facts, but without a context of specific events, and thus without meaning to the word. Thus it appears in a central passage of Heidegger's *Sein und Zeit,* see *is.* Another example is found on the first page of Ayer's *The Problem of Knowledge:*

> 'Philosophical theories are not tested by observation. They are neutral with respect to particular matters of fact. This is not to say that philosophers are not concerned with facts, but they are in the strange position that all the evidence which bears upon their problems is already available to them. It is not further scientific information that is needed to decide such philosophical questions as whether the material world is real, whether objects continue to exist at times when they are not perceived, whether other human beings are conscious in the same sense as one is oneself.'

These passages confirm how the Aristotelian program of philosophy is fully alive until this day. See also *consciousness, existence, is, philosophy, reality.*

Farrington, Benjamin: See *Aristotle.*

Favrholdt David: See *mathematical logic.*

Feeling: Nothing is more foolish than the philosophers' lack of understanding of feelings. This is closely related to their adoration of logic. As ordinarily presented in a philosophical context, feelings are an unreliable, wild element of immature persons, an element the truth-seeking philosopher has ascended above (see e.g. *truth,* quotations from Eddington).

As described by William James any *thought object* embraces feelings (see *stream of thought*). We cannot turn our attention to anything without becoming affected by feelings. Feelings are simply a part of every thought object. The feeling may be in the fringe of the objects, but may also become the core of the object, that towards which our *attention* is turned. When we think of a beloved person our thought must necessarily have feelings of love. We may then turn our thought a bit and ask ourselves what is in this loving feeling, how it is constituted.

31

Feeling ...

Our feelings are multiple beyond any limits and go entirely beyond what we are able to describe, even just approximately, by the poor vocabulary at our ordinary command. Certain feelings, those that one tends to think of first, for example grief, hatred, enthusiasm, have a strong influence on our overall state. Most feelings are less prominent, but they are of decisive importance by influencing our attention, and thus which parts of the present thought object we will deal with. We tend to ignore what gives us feelings of boredom and weariness, and give attention to whatever arouses our interest, gives us delight, tickles us.

The experience of *being acquainted* with something is a feeling. The experience of something as *real* is a feeling.

Certain feelings contribute strongly to directing the stream of thought, influencing the *associations*, q.v. Thus William James talks about *feelings of tendency* and *feelings of aching void*. Feelings of tendency enter into thoughts about unsolved problems. An example of a feeling of aching void is that which is prominent when trying to recall a forgotten name.

Even if philosophers do not willingly talk about feelings there is no reason to assume that they do not experience feelings, like other people. Thus for example there are clear indications that the thought of *mathematical logic* in many philosophers is accompanied by feelings of respect and awe. I also have feelings about mathematical logic. They are rather different, though, about the same that I have for scarecrows, for crude sticks dressed up with a worn-out jacket in order scare the birds.

See also *acquaintance, introspection*. Further references are given in the Literature Appendix.

Force: See *Newtonian mechanics.*

Formal language: In certain contexts, such as the academic pursuit of computing, there is a prominent tendency to emphasize something called formal languages. However, in this there is nothing clearly delimited or particularly important. The concern at hand is to achieve a description of certain matters, and this, like any description, has to build upon a choice of descriptive elements. In such contexts it is often found that the descriptive purpose may be served by formulating descriptions in terms of specially selected words, symbols, and graphical styles. Typical examples from daily life are found in train tables, where both the words and the symbols, and the way they are arranged in tables, have to be understood in a certain manner, as descriptions of the train traffic.

In describing certain types of complicated structures, e.g. programs for the control of computers, it is necessary to use correspondingly complicated styles of writing. A formal language is collection of ways of writing, usually of such a form that the descriptions may be written in ordinary typography, that is as sequences of characters arranged in lines. A style of writing of this form, used to control computers, is called a *programming language*. Such a form of description is introduced by a special explanation or definition, either separately or as a part of the description.

The designations 'formal language' and 'programming language' in this connection are misleading in so far as they by analogy make a false suggestion that ordinary linguistic activity should build upon a fixed set of ways of expression having definite meanings, see *language-as-something-fallacy* and *language-rule-fallacy*. Further references are given in the Literature Appendix.

Foundations (of sciences): Philosophy constantly exerts a misleading influence upon the academic teaching through the talk about 'sciences' and their 'foundations'. A picture is painted of various 'sciences', in which they are presented as a number of separate units, each having its 'foundations'.

The philosophical talk of 'sciences' and their 'foundations', and the origin of this talk in Aristotle's talk of what 'is', is presented explicitly by Heidegger in *Sein und Zeit,* p. 8f, under the heading 'The ontological primacy of the question of being'. He writes:

> 'Being is always the being of a being. The whole of the being may according to its various realms become the field of a liberation and encircling of definite domains. ... Scientific research accomplishes the clarification and first affirmation of the domain in a naive and rough manner. ... The 'basic notions' that emerge in this way at first remain the guide for the first concrete enclosure of the domain. Even though the main emphasis of the research always resides in this positivity, its genuine progress does not fulfil itself so much in the collection of results and the presentation of them in "handbooks", as in the questioning about the foundation of the domain in question, which is driven forward by the increasing insight into the matters.
> The genuine 'movements' of the sciences take place in the revisions of the foundations, revisions that may be more or less radical and that are not transparent to the sciences themselves. The level of a science is determined by whether it is *capable* of a crisis of its foundations.'

Here we have a clear expression of the relation of philosophy to science. Philosophically we have to talk about definite 'sciences' and their 'levels'. What really matters are the 'foundations', with a special plus to a field that can show us a 'crisis of its foundations'. All the investigations and descriptions of ever more phenomena is of no philosophical interest. Take for example fields like chemistry, astronomy, or geology. They have neither foundations nor crises of their foundations. Evidently they are philosophically poor fields at a low scientific level. The investigations in chemistry of new substances and their properties, and the development of new substances for numerous applications, e.g. medicines, all what is collected in what Heidegger calls 'handbooks', is just insignificant. These kinds of things are of no interest to the philosopher, who has slaves to attend to all that is practical.

For Heidegger there is only interest in 'foundations' and their 'crises'. His saying this of course has an impressive air of insight, but if we are impolite and look closer at Heidegger's talk about such crises, we may find that the insight displayed is less than impressive. Thus Heidegger talks about 'the fight between formalism and intuitionism' in mathematics and 'the theory of relativity' in physics. Claiming that these have a similarity in being 'foundations crises' is empty verbiage.

Later in his section about 'The ontological primacy of the question of being' Heidegger continues:

'Basic concepts are the specifications in which the underlying domain of all the thematic objects of a science achieves the understanding of all past and positive investigations. These concepts obtain their proper indication and 'justification' only subsequent to a corresponding previous exploration of the domain itself. But in so far as each of these domains has been extracted from the realm of the being itself, such previous creative exploration of the basic concepts means nothing other than presentation of this being upon the basic constitution of its being. Such exploration must precede the positive sciences; and this it *can do*. The works by *Plato* and *Aristotle* prove it.'

Yes, this he writes, Heidegger, in his philosophical presumption! '... presentation of this being upon the basic constitution of its being', this is what he writes, translated from '... Auslegung dieses Seienden auf die Grundverfassung seines Seins': claptrap.

And this, says Heidegger, is what Plato and Aristotle have presented in their works. It did not have much luck, what they presented in this way, though. The sciences were virtually dead for centuries after their time and only came back to life when Aristotle had been rejected by Galileo.

Even though the philosophers' talk about separate sciences and their foundations works its enchantment over many scientists, other voices may also be heard, however. Thus Einstein speaks quite differently. At the beginning of an article titled *Physics and Reality* he says: 'The whole of science is nothing more than a refinement of everyday thinking'. He continues this line of thought in more detail in a later article titled *The Fundaments of Theoretical Physics* where he says:

'The scientific way of forming concepts differs from that which we use in our daily life, not basically, but merely in the more precise definition of concepts and conclusions; ... from the very beginning there has always been present the attempt to find a unifying theoretical basis for all these single sciences, consisting of a minimum of concepts and fundamental relationships, from which all the concepts and relationships of the single disciplines might be derived by logical process. This is what we mean by the search for a foundation of the whole of physics. ... From what has been said it is clear that the word foundations in this connection does not mean something analogous in all respects to the foundations of a building. Logically considered, of course, the various single laws of physics rest upon this foundation. But whereas a building may be seriously damaged by a heavy storm or spring flood, yet its foundations remain intact, in science the logical foundation is always in greater peril from new experiences or new knowledge than are the branch disciplines with their closer experimental contacts. In the connection of the foundation with all the single parts lies its great significance, but likewise its greatest danger in face of any new factor.'

The talk of definite fields and their foundations is a misunderstanding of the scientific activity. It often happens that significant contributions cannot be placed within one definite field or any 'science'. As just one example, does Watson and Crick's epoch-making work on the structure of DNA belong to chemistry, or biology, or genetics? Nobody can tell: the question is insignificant (about this work see also *scientific-scholarly activity*). The matter was clearly expressed by Edgar Rubin (*Videnskab* in Salmonsens Konversationsleksikon, 1928):

'The classification of the sciences and the mutual division between the sciences are often being vehemently discussed, because it is believed that they are matters of profound, scientific issues, while it is far more historical and practical concerns that here are and have to be decisive.'

As one example of such a practical concern the organization of universities may be mentioned.

See also *mathematical analysis, description.* Further references are given in the Literature Appendix.

Franklin, Rosalyn: See *scientific-scholarly activity.*

Freud, Sigmund: See *philosophy of science, Popper.*

Fringe: The word is used here as by William James to denote an aspect of the thought objects experienced in our stream of thought. See *acquaintance, association, introspection, language, psychology, stream of thought.*

Galileo Galilæi: See *Aristotle, foundations.*

Gauss, Carl Friedrich: See *philosophy of science.*

Geology: See *philosophy of science.*

Gödel, Kurt: See *mathematical logic.*

Grammar: The school masters like to maintain that we must know the rules of grammar in order to be able to speak correctly. Such talk is misleading in several ways. A set of rules of grammar is descriptive of a certain language style. To know such rules is important only to a person who wishes to express himself or herself in another style than one of those he or she is already used to. Most commonly the matter is that the person, who like anybody else is used to expressing himself or herself in one of a number of verbal styles, wishes or is given the task to become familiar with an impersonal written style. A corresponding situation prevails when the person wishes to become fluent in a foreign language. In such situations it may be useful to be introduced to the new style through a description of it.

The mistake is to claim that these useful forms of learning praxis should support the idea that the mental process of conversation involves grammatical rules.

See also *language-rule-fallacy.* Further references are given in the Literature Appendix.

Habit: As stressed by William James (*Principles of Psychology,* chapter IV *Habit*) one of the most striking things about living creatures as seen from outside is that they are bundles of habits. Also the linguistic activity and the *stream of thought* (q.v.) we each of us experience are entirely dominated by habits.

See also *association, belief, disposition, knowledge, language, psychology.* Further references are given in the Literature Appendix.

Hartnack, Justus: See *concept.*

Heidegger, Martin: See *foundations, is.*

Hume, David: See *psychology.*

Høffding, Harald: See *–ism.*

Idealism: *Dictionary of Philosophy* explains idealism in this way: 'Any system or doctrine whose fundamental interpretative principle is ideal. Broadly, any theoretical or practical view emphasizing mind (soul, spirit, life) or what is characteristically of pre-eminent value or significance to it. Negatively, the alternative to Materialism.' Correspondingly an idealist is explained philosophically to be a person who adopts idealism.

All this to me is without clear meaning. How a person might adopt, or emphasize, something that might be called a 'fundamental interpretative principle' is obscure to me. I myself refuse to be hooked on such a peg. It appears to me that what a person emphasizes in some point of view must be totally dependent upon what the point of view is about. As to myself I emphasize mind *when it is relevant.* But even so I may emphasize other matters in other contexts.

This very talk of a 'fundamental interpretative principle' reveals an assumption about the way people think. The use of the word 'fundamental' in this context only makes sense as a metaphor, since there is no talk about buildings and their fundaments. What is fundamental in this context must thus be certain claims and statements that in what is said function as a point of departure, in the sense that everything else emerges as its consequences. In other words, everything else must have a connection with the fundament as through a logical derivation. But if this picture is to correspond to a person's way of thinking, it must be assumed that this thought activity may be described as logical inferences from a fundament. This is an assumption that cannot in any manner be confirmed by direct observation of people's stream of thought, since the stream of thought is an even flow, without atoms that might enter into a logical derivation, see *association, perception, stream of thought.*

The assumption is not either confirmed by the statements made by the philosophers. By a bit of attentive reading one will find that even the most famous philosophers make pronouncements that lack coherence, see e.g. *Descartes,* and statements made by Russell, quoted under *perception.*

Induction: See *philosophy of science.*

Inference: See *logic.*

Inference rule: See *mathematical logic.*

Integral calculus: See *mathematical analysis.*

Intelligence: 'Intelligence' together with 'knowledge' are prominent examples of how an unfortunate choice of descriptive elements may lead a field of description astray. Both terms are used in descriptions of individual persons, in such a way that it is said that knowledge and intelligence are things a person may possess. Both terms give rise to endless, unavailing debates of what they denote. As particularly concerns intelligence it is spoken about as a property of each person, something that the person may possess in greater or smaller quantity or degree. This way of speaking meets the empirical fact that a closer study of practically any outstanding personality shows that the same person who in one context has acted highly intelligently, in other contexts has behaved stupidly. Thus the word intelligence is useless for describing properties of persons.

Intentionalism: Defined in *Dictionary of Philosophy* as theory of mind and knowledge which considers intentionality a distinctive if not the defining characteristic of mind and basis for mind's cognitive and conative functions. This explanation is unclear by its talk about 'knowledge'. See also –*ism, knowing, knowledge.*

Introspection: By introspection is meant that a person directs his or her attention at his or her *stream of thought* (q.v.), rather than at that with which the thought objects are acquainted. Introspection happens regularly in presumably most people. For example is it only after introspection that a person may find expression for pleasure or displeasure at something the person has perceived through the senses, sight, hearing, taste, touch, smell. Only after introspection will we exclaim, what delicious wine! Only through introspection do we become acquainted with the stream of thought and its ever changing contents.

As illustration I may say something about how I through introspection may arrive at a description of my linguistic formulation activity. This activity is in full swing at this moment while I am pressing the keys of my computer. By being specially attentive I may follow the steps of my thought that lead to the text appearing on the screen. Thus I am able to ascertain that my typing activity is prepared by my *imagining* certain words and phrases. These images appear in my thought objects as speech that I hear in my inner ear, in my own voice. When I start to write a new passage I thus hear some of the words that I may perhaps use. They come to me, I do not know how, when I put myself into an expectant mood, and when I am undisturbed and rested.

This steady development of my stream of thought may be described as a continued series of *associations*. As soon as words have come to me my state changes, in such a way that I can turn my attention towards the thought objects that the words through association call forth in my stream of thought. In the fringe of these objects there are both images and feelings that are related to my understanding of the words. These enter into my consideration of how the words approach to expressing my insight, my subject.

This insight itself, when I start a sentence, is not expressed in words or otherwise sensible. It may be described as a *feeling of tendency* in a certain direction. Often several (words) phrases (come) appear in my thought at the same time. Then I let (consider) (happens) in my thought the phrases act upon me, one after the other; I let the *fringe* of faint feelings of the secondary meanings of the words that accompany each of them act (get a hearing) in my thought. To illustrate what I have just said, I have in the sentences just written, in parentheses inserted some of the phrases I have considered, but have decided not to use.

With the dominance of *behaviorism,* introspection has become a taboo in psychology.

Further references are given in the Literature Appendix.

Introspective method: This phrase enters into the philosophers' explanations of certain –*ism*s (q.v.). The very phrase 'introspective method' implies the fallacy that introspection is something that one may or may not choose to adopt. As described under *introspection* (q.v.), introspection happens regularly in presumably all people. What may or may not be chosen is to talk about introspection. But even the behaviorists who refuse to talk about it reveal that they experience introspection. How otherwise do they know that they are so hostile to talking about introspection?

Intuitionism: Defined in *Dictionary of Philosophy* as any philosophy in which intuition is appealed to as the basis of knowledge, or at least of philosophical knowledge. The notion becomes unclear through the talk about 'knowledge'. See also *–ism, knowing, knowledge*.

Is: A great deal of the philosophers' talk is centered around metaphysics, more specifically locutions that contain the words 'is', 'be', and 'being'. Thus these words enter into the philosophers' explanations of certain *–isms*. In this philosophical talk there is much unclarity, deriving mostly from the fact that 'is' in ordinary ways of talking is the most common and at the same time the most ambiguous word there is, and partly from the philosophers' tendency to succumb to the fallacy that each word corresponds to something definite that the word means (see *word-as-code-of-meaning-fallacy*).

One example of the mist around 'is' has been given in the article about *Descartes*. A rich collection of nonsense around the word 'is' may be found in Heidegger's *Sein und Zeit* (*Being and Time*). Heidegger right from his initial quotation from Plato's *Sophist* places himself directly in the wake of the Aristotelian line. The quotation is:

> 'For evidently you have already for a long time been familiar with what you mean when you use the expression "being", while we for a time thought we understood it, but now we have become embarrassed.'

Heidegger continues to ask whether we today have an answer to what we mean by the word 'being'. To this he answers directly: by no means.

With this way of speaking Heidegger without further ado has made the assumption that each word, e.g. 'being', corresponds to a definite meaning, whatever this may mean. But this is an entirely unjustified assumption (see *word-as-code-of-meaning-fallacy*). The words we use obtain a meaning to us at each use of them. This meaning appears as a part of a thought object (see *stream of thought*), and thus is personal and ephemeral.

After a discussion of some objections to speaking about being, Heidegger on page 5 arrives at the core of the matter:

> 'As [expression of] search the questioning [about the meaning of being] requires a previous guidance from what is being searched. The meaning of being must thus in a way be already available to us. As suggestion: we are always moving in an understanding of being. Out of this grows the explicit questioning about the meaning of being and the tendency towards this concept. We do not *know* what 'being' says. But already when we ask "What *is* 'being'?" we remain in an understanding of "is", without being able to affirm conceptually what the "is" means. We even do not know the horizon within which we might conceive and affirm the meaning. *This average and vague understanding of being is a fact.*'

To this passage I can say for my part that I do not see the sense of asking "What *is* 'being'?", and so I feel alien to the rest of the talk. What is this fact that Heidegger, emphasized in italics, takes as the point of departure of his whole book, where does it come from, who is acquainted with it, by what experience? From where comes the average he talks about, out of which manifold has it been formed? All this is entirely unclear, so his fact appears merely as a postulate. In other words, I do not know what he is talking about. The whole passage I can only see as an attempt to seduce me into accepting misty talk.

The philosophical claim that 'is' has a definite meaning in our understanding of the world is in strange contrast, both to the use of any other word and to the ordinary use of 'is' in particular. As anyone may discover, 'is' is used with several quite different meanings. In certain contexts 'is' connects the denotation of a thing with a descriptive expression for it: 'The train is late', 'she is hungry'. In other contexts the connection is to a denotation: 'His name is Smith'. In yet other connections the word is put between two expressions that in certain contexts may replace one another: 'two plus two is four'.

Part of the philosophical nonsense around 'is' is related to the Aristotelian belief in *essential properties*. This is often encountered in pseudo-significant statements, such as for example: Man is a thinking/rational animal; man is a molecular-biological/information processing/physical-chemical/ ... system; man is a ghost in a machine. The nonsense in these statements is related to taking 'is' as a short form of 'has as its essential property to be', i.e. the statements are understood as follows: Man has as his essential property to be a thinking/rational animal; ...

The nonsense in these forms of statements is difficult to discern, because of the unclarity that comes with the many ways of using 'is'. The point is that each of the statements might readily be taken to be descriptive, that is as though 'is' should be understood as 'may from a certain point of view be described as'. This would give us: Man may from a certain point of view be described as a thinking/rational animal; man may from a certain point of view be described as a molecular-biological/information processing/physical-chemical/ ... system; man may from a certain point of view be described as a ghost in a machine. As descriptions are neither right or wrong, only more or less adequate and coherent with other descriptions, each of these statements may have a useful meaning.

See also *Descartes, description, essence, foundations, –ism, knowing, necessity, perception, science, scientific-scholarly activity, thinking-as-language-fallacy.*

–ism: Present-day philosophical discussions consist for a large part in tagging labels, –isms, on people, understood as a summary of their views. In a discussion with a philosopher one tries perhaps to express a view of some controversial question. As the reaction one then gets: 'Aha, you are an x-ist', where x has to replaced by some designation. And so the philosopher is satisfied; he (yes, he, I have never encountered or heard of a woman philosopher, women have too much good sense to engage in such)—he has put you into a box with a label on it, and so the matter to him has been settled. Philosophers also put such labels upon themselves. For example Høffding in *Dictionary of Philosophy* is classified as a cautious idealistic monist, while he called himself a critical monist.

Thus it may be foreseen that if a philosopher takes upon himself to express a stand towards what I write in this dictionary, the reaction will be: there writes an antiphilosophist.

There are many –isms for philosophers to take care of, so they are kept busy. Thus in *Dictionary of Philosophy* we find: absolutism, accidentalism, acosmism, activism, agnosticism, animism, Aristotelianism, atomism, automatism, Benthamism, Berkeleianism, Cartesianism, conceptual realism, conscientalism, determinism, (scientific) empiricism, experimentalism, finalism, Hegelianism, Herbartism, hylomorphism, hylotheism, hylozoism, (critical, epistemological, conceptual, monistic, moral, objective, personal, Platonic, pluralistic, psychological, pure, realistic, subjective, transcendental, unpersonal) idealism, illusionism, individualism, instrumentalism, intentionalism, introspectionism, intuitionism, Jansenism, Jesuitism, Kantianism, libertarianism, materialism, mechanism, mentalism, monergism, (epistemological, critical, neutral) monism, nativism, naturalism, necessitarianism, neutralism, nominalism, (pan-) objectivism, occasionalism, Ockhamism, ontologism, panlogism, phenomenalism, physicalism, Platonism, pluralism, positivism, rationalism, (axiological, critical, epistemological, natural, neo–, representative) realism, (epistemological, objective) relativism, scepticism, sensationalism, solipsism, spiritualism, subjectivism, transcendentalism, tychism, voluntarism.

The rest of us have no reason to torture ourselves with all these –isms, however, since they do not denote anything clearly. They are all explained in *Dictionary of Philosophy* in terms of a much smaller number of words, *but these words are used by philosophers outside a context that might make them meaningful.* These words are the following, that are commented upon in this Dictionary: *(effective) cause, determinism, essence, existence, fact, introspective method, is, knowledge, language of science, laws of physics* (see *physics*), *matter, (logic, causal) necessity, objectivity, reality, soul, substance, (physical) thing, (absolute) truth, will, (physical, objective) world.*

As characteristic examples of how philosophers explain the –isms they talk about, see *epistemological relativism, idealism, intentionalism, intuitionism, mentalism, monism, nativism, occasionalism, phenomenalism.*

The talk about *-ists* corresponding to the –isms invites to a critical remark. If it is to make sense to tag an -ist-label onto a person it must be assumed that the person's stand in all kinds of questions may be derived logically from a single principle, that principle which is denoted by the –ism. This would depend on the notion that each person's thinking is coherent. But this is a totally unjustified assumption, see *idealism.*

A philosopher's adherence to one of the –isms seems to be a matter of taste. Some like realism, others formalism, and yet others positivism, just as some like coffee, others tea.

See also *knowing, language-as-something-fallacy, soul.*

-ist: See *–ism.*

James, William: James in his *Principles of Psychology* from 1890 presented a descriptive account of the human mental activity. The work rejects the dominant thought-as-perception-mistake and the Aristotelian logic and atomism in the description of the thought activity. See *association, association by similarity, attention, concept, concept-is-word-fallacy, feeling, fringe, habit, knowing, mathematical logic, language-as-something-fallacy, perception, psychology, reality, reasoning, stream of thought, thing, thought-as-perception-mistake.*

Further references are given in the Literature Appendix.

Jespersen, Otto: See *language-as-something-fallacy, logic, word-as-code-of-meaning-fallacy*. Further references are given in the Literature Appendix.

Joyce, James: See *stream of thought.*

Kjørup, Søren: See *existence, language-as-something-fallacy, Wittgenstein.*

know-how: If a computer were to be made to simulate human intelligent behavior, the control of that behavior would have to be expressible in rules. In other words, it would be necessary that *know-how* could be based upon *knowing that.* The impossibility of this has been shown by Gilbert Ryle, on p. 31 of *The Concept of Mind*:

> 'The crucial objection to the intellectualist legend is this. The consideration of propositions is itself an operation the execution of which can be more or less intelligent, less or more stupid. But if, for any operation to be intelligently executed, a prior theoretical operation had first to be performed and performed intelligently, it would be a logical impossibility for anyone ever to break into the circle.
>
> Let us consider some salient points at which this regress would arise. According to the legend, whenever an agent does anything intelligently, his act is preceded and steered by another internal act of considering a regulative proposition appropriate to his practical problem. But what makes him consider the one maxim which is appropriate rather than any of the thousands which are not? Why does the hero not find himself calling to mind a cooking-recipe, or a rule of Formal Logic? Perhaps he does, but then his intellectual process is silly and not sensible.'

Further references are given in the Literature Appendix.

Knowing: 'Knowledge' is one of the most frequently used words in the philosophers' vocabulary. The word appears in the explanations of many of their *–isms*, see for example *epistemological relativism, intentionalism, intuitionism, phenomenalism*. But it is a word whose meaning in philosophical contexts is so unclear that, like 'logic', it is useless.

For example Bertrand Russell in his book *The Analysis of Mind* used the word 'knowledge' on practically every page. At the beginning of lecture IX he says that 'The analysis of knowledge will occupy us until the end of the thirteenth lecture, and is the most difficult part of our whole enterprise.' In lecture XIII, Truth and Falsehood, he says: 'We wish to believe that our beliefs, sometimes at least, yield *knowledge*, and a belief does not yield knowledge unless it is true.' But what Russell here is talking about is veiled in a mist.

Quine talks about 'knowledge' in an unclear manner which is characteristic of him. Thus in *Quiddities* he starts his article about 'knowledge' by saying that 'Knowledge is true belief'. One page later he then says: 'I think that for scientific or philosophical purposes the best we can do is give up the notion of knowledge as a bad job ...'.

Ayer has written a book titled *The Problem of Knowledge*. He starts his Preface by saying that his book is an example of a philosophical enquiry. On the first page of the text he then says that philosophers are preoccupied with the essential nature of things (see *essence*). Thus he clearly adheres to the tradition of Aristotle.

Ayer's book does not speak well for philosophy, it is unclear and nonsensical. Even just the title may be a warning to the reader. What is the problem he is talking about? Ordinary sensible people are not acquainted with any problem of knowing. They know perfectly well how one talks about something they themselves or other people know, they every day make use of what they or other people know, and they know by experience that one is sometimes mistaken, that something one thought one knew turns out to be wrong, and that one may not succeed with something one thought one knew how to do.

After the brief introduction about what philosophy is, Ayer spends the first pages of his book discussing what, if anything, might be common to the ways the word 'knowledge' is used in ordinary talking. His program becomes clear when on page 12 he writes:

'If knowledge were always knowledge that something is the case, then such a common factor might be found in the existence of a common relation to truth.'

Ayer continues to discuss various possible objections to this program. He presents examples: 'A dog knows its master, a baby knows its mother', where, as he says, 'they do not know any statements to be true.' He then continues in vague terms:

'There is a sense in which knowing something, in this usage of the term, is always a matter of knowing what it is; and in this sense it can perhaps be represented as knowing a fact, as knowing that something is so.'

With this last formulation we have arrived at one of the favourite inanities of philosophers, the use of verbal phrases containing 'is' without further specification of what, see *is*. And so Ayer has arrived at the crucial point.

Let us summarize: So as to be able to say that knowledge always is a matter of something being the case, Ayer has to say that when a dog knows its master it means that the dog knows that its master is. Thus the dog must possess an understanding saying that the statement 'my master is' is true. But in order to understand that the statement is true the dog must first understand what the statement 'my master is' says. But clearly that is possible only if the dog knows that 'my master' who is spoken of in the statement. But according to Ayer it was precisely in order to know 'my master' that the dog had to understand the statement. Thus Ayer's whole presentation is arguing along an impossible circle. *It does not hang together to claim that knowing is a matter of understanding the truth of a statement.*

A common feature of the philosophers' talk about knowledge is that it builds on the notion that it makes sense to talk of knowledge as a kind of matter or substance, and the human mind as a container for this kind of matter (see also *knowledge*). These notions entirely lack justification in a more detailed description of how the human mental activity works. But after the behaviorists have taken over in psychology, the mental activity has become taboo. It is declared to be unscientific to talk of the activity of thought, such as it is experienced by everybody in each of our wake moments. Thus is has become impossible to talk about how that which in everyday talk is denoted 'to know something' may be understood in the context of that activity.

The philosophers pay no attention to the fact that knowing, whatever it is, necessarily has to be understood as something related to people's activity of thought, that it has to build upon a psychological *description* of people's mental life.

But philosophers are not interested in describing. When they talk about knowledge they invariably cling to questions of logic, of truth. They use the word knowledge without further explanation, without showing a context that might give the word meaning, for example a context that tells what are the matters of concern of the knowledge talked about. A large number of the –isms the philosophers are so fond of, are explained in terms of the word knowledge without further explanation, see *–ism*.

Philosophers appear to be totally ignorant of the most characteristic features of the human thought activity. They seem never to have heard about the two central aspects of knowing that are displayed clearly in most Western languages, except English, corresponding to the phrases *'be acquainted with' / 'know about'*. A person may be acquainted with all sorts of things he or she knows little about. Perhaps I am acquainted with the man in the drug store around the corner from where I live. I may perhaps have seen him many times and may occasionally have bought a sandwich from him. But perhaps I know very little about him. Perhaps I do not know his name or anything about his life outside the drug store.

The philosophers' misunderstandings concerning knowing are displayed clearly in *Dictionary of Philosophy*, in the explanation of Acquaintance, Knowledge by: 'The apprehension of a quality, thing or person which is in the direct presence of the knowing subject.' This explanation shows a total misunderstanding of the fundamentally important aspect of human thought that William James denotes *knowledge by acquaintance*, see below. The misleading explanation seems to have been copied directly from Bertrand Russell's article *Knowledge by Acquaintance and Knowledge by Description,* in which the misunderstanding is presented in the first words:

'The object of the following paper is to consider what it is that we know in cases where we know propositions about "the so-and-so" without knowing who or what the so-and-so is. For example, I know that the candidate who gets most votes will be elected, though I do not know who is the candidate who will get most votes.'

The inanity in this passage resides in the formulations 'we know propositions about "the so-and-so"' and 'without knowing who or what the so-and-so is'. Statements about 'the so-and-so' where we *are not acquainted with* 'the so-and-so' are nonsense to us, and thus it is nonsense to talk about that we 'know propositions about "the so-and-so" without knowing who or what the so-and-so is'.

That which a person may be said to *know about something*, that which perhaps may be either correct or wrong, true or false, depends entirely upon the person being already *acquainted with that something*. Thus if I am asked if I know the time of departure of the train we will take, if the question is to make sense at all I must be acquainted with the train we will take.

The philosophical confusion around knowing ought to be a matter of the past. Knowing has been described with brilliant clarity by William James in 1890. Below are a few pages from his *Principles of Psychology* that ought so lie under every philosopher's night pillow (vol. I, p. 216 - 222):

'Now the *relation of knowing* is the most mysterious thing in the world. If we ask how one thing *can* know another we are led into the heart of *Erkenntnisstheorie* and metaphysics. The psychologist, for his part, does not consider the matter so curiously as this. Finding a world before him which he cannot but believe that *he* knows, and setting himself to study his own past thoughts, or someone else's thoughts, of what he believes to be that same world; he cannot but conclude that those other thoughts know it after their fashion even as he knows it after his. Knowledge becomes for him an ultimate relation that must be admitted, whether it be explained or not, just like difference or resemblance, which no one seeks to explain. ... *The psychologist's attitude toward cognition* will be so important in the sequel that we must not leave it until it is made perfectly clear. *It is a thoroughgoing dualism.* It supposes two elements, mind knowing and thing known, and treats them as irreducible. ...

There are two kinds of knowledge broadly and practically distinguishable: we may call them respectively *knowledge of acquaintance* and *knowledge-about*. Most languages express the distinction; thus γνωναι, ειδεναι; *noscere, scire; kennen, wissen; connaître, savoir.* I am acquainted with many people and things, which I know very little about, except their presence in the places where I have met them. I know the color blue when I see it, and the flavor of a pear when I taste it; I know an inch when I move my finger through it; a second of time, when I feel it pass; an effort of attention when I notice it; but *about* the inner nature of these facts or what makes them what they are, I can say nothing at all. I cannot impart acquaintance with them to any one who has not already made it himself. I cannot *describe* them, make a blind man guess what blue is like, define to a child a syllogism, or tell a philosopher in just what respect distance is just what it is, and differs from other forms of relation. At most, I can say to my friends, Go to certain places and act in certain ways, and these objects will probably come. All the elementary natures of the world, its highest genera, the simple qualities of matter and mind, together with the kinds of relation that subsist between them, must either not be known at all, or known in this dumb way of acquaintance without *knowledge-about*. In minds able to speak at all there is, it is true, *some* knowledge about everything. Things can at least be classed, and the times of their appearance told. But in general, the less we analyze a thing, and the fewer of its relations we perceive, the less we know about it and the more our familiarity with it is of the acquaintance-type. The two types of knowledge are, therefore, as the human mind practically exerts them, relative terms. That is, the same thought of a thing may be called knowledge-about it in comparison with a simpler thought, or acquaintance with it in comparison with a thought of it that is more articulate and explicit still.

The grammatical sentence expresses this. Its 'subject' stands for an object of acquaintance which, by the addition of the predicate, is to get something known about it. We may already know a good deal, when we hear the subject named—its name may have rich connotations. But, know we much or little then, we know more still when the sentence is done. We can relapse at will into a mere condition of acquaintance with an object by scattering our attention and staring at it in a vacuous trance-like way. We can ascend to knowledge *about* it by rallying our wits and proceeding to notice and analyze and think. What we are only acquainted with is only *present* to our minds; we *have* it, or the idea of it. But when we know about it, we do more than merely have it; we seem, as we think over its relations, to subject it to a sort of *treatment* and to *operate* upon it with our thought. The words feeling and thought give voice to the antithesis. Through feeling we become acquainted with things, but only by our thoughts do we know about them. Feelings are the germ and starting point of cognition, thoughts the developed tree. The minimum of grammatical subject, of objective presence, of reality known about, the mere beginning of knowledge, must be named by the word that says the least. Such a word is the interjection, as *lo! there! ecco! voilá!* or the article or demonstrative pronoun introducing the sentence, *the, it, that.*'

Further descriptions of what we mean when we talk about knowing have been presented by Austin and Ryle. They both build their understanding of the human way of thinking upon what in meaningful ordinary talking may be said about it. Thus Austin in *Other Minds* asks what are sensible forms of answer from a person whose knowledge about a particular, current, empirical fact is challenged. Austin writes:

'Suppose I have said 'There's a bittern at the bottom of the garden', and you ask 'How do you know?' my reply may take very different forms:
(*a*) I was brought up in the Fens
(*b*) I heard it
(*c*) The keeper reported it
(*d*) By its booming
(*e*) From the booming noise
(*f*) Because it's booming.
We may say, roughly, that the first three are answers to the questions 'How do you come to know?' 'How are you in a position to know?' or 'How do *you* know?' understood in different ways: while the other three are answers to 'How can you tell?' understood in different ways. That is, I may take you to have been asking:
(1) How do I come to be in a position to know about bitterns?
(2) How do I come to be in a position to say there's a bittern here and now?
(3) How do (can) I tell bitterns?
(4) How do (can) I tell the thing here and now as a bittern?
The implication is that in order to know this is a bittern, I must have
(1) been trained in an environment where I could become familiar with bitterns
(2) had a certain opportunity in the current case
(3) learned to recognize or tell bitterns
(4) succeeded in recognizing or telling this as a bittern.
(1) and (2) mean that my experience must have been of certain kinds, that I must have had certain opportunities: (3) and (4) mean that I must have exerted a certain kind and amount of acumen.'

Each of these answers may be seen as an expression that knowing is a matter of reacting by *habit*, on the basis of *dispositions* that have been acquired by training in the past. Some of the answers tell how the habits were trained ('brought up in the Fens'), others make clear that the habitual reaction was applicable in the current situation. Some of the habits involve words of the language ('The keeper reported it'), others are matters of others forms of personal reaction.

Knowing ...

Ryle has described the dispositions that are commonly denoted 'to know something', particularly in a comparison with those that are denoted 'to believe something', see *belief.*

See also *concept, perception, psychology, reality, stream of thought, truth.* Further references are given in the Literature Appendix.

Knowing by acquaintance: See *acquaintance, knowing by.*

Knowledge: A large part of the philosophical inanity involves a form of description of people in which the word knowledge is used to denote a *something* of some kind. The nonsense arises when the word knowledge releases the reaction: aha, knowledge, that is something that one may keep, transfer, and classify into various sorts. As a consequence of the knowledge-nonsense there is much talk about such myths as knowledge representation and the knowledge society.

All this nonsense may be avoided only by not talking about knowledge at all, but rather instead about *knowing*, q.v.

The knowledge-nonsense is often related to a confusion of something human beings acquire in the course of their lives on the one hand, and *descriptions* on the other. A fallacy that the human mind is a container of descriptions is thriving. The fallacy of this notion is evident to anyone who tries to generate descriptions, as most writers do. As any writer knows the descriptions do no just come forth, as a copying from a container in the mind. Each word has to be squeezed forth during an often tiresome lying in wait (see the description under *introspection*).

That which for each person is the precondition of his or her knowing reactions are *habits, dispositions*, qq.v.

See also *–ism, stream of thought, nonsense.* Further references are given in the Literature Appendix.

Kuhn, Thomas: See *paradigm.*

Language: A large part of the philosophical inanity is related to untenable notions about the human linguistic activity, see *language-fallacy.*

The talk of various languages, for example Danish, Swedish, and English, evidently originated in the well known fact that while people have no difficulty in speaking with those among whom they have grown up, they cannot similarly talk with people from other parts of the world. The speech sounds that are used in one location are different from those used in other places. To this is added the equally well known fact that the young children cannot talk during their first years, but that they only gradually, over a period of years, acquire the manner of speaking of the adults.

But then a shift in the talk about language occurs. It is implied that language is a kind of substance that the individual person receives and possesses. Further one talks about correct language. It is said that even though persons mostly speak without any difficulty with whomever they like, particularly their close relatives, they often speak wrongly, incorrectly. Then the school masters come into the picture, and the fight with, and against, the school children begins.

The philosophers' talk about language is illustrated clearly in Wittgenstein's *Philosophische Betrachtungen* (see *word-as-code-of-meaning-fallacy*). What Wittgenstein here says about words and language is psychologically hopeless. Wittgenstein makes first a tacit assumption that the linguistic activity is a specific and peculiar addition to any other mental activity of the person. That other activity is hardly mentioned by Wittgenstein, and its relation to what he takes to be the linguistic activity remains totally obscure.

Wittgenstein's way of speaking depends on the further assumption that the word language denotes something definite, a set of words having definite meanings.

Wittgenstein forgets that all human mental activity is entirely dependent upon the person's momentary situation. This holds in particular of the meaning we, in our thought, attach to the words we hear or read. That this is the case is particularly visible with the most frequently used words, for example he, she, it. These words will in the course of an ordinary conversation be used with many different meanings. Which meaning holds at each use is perceived by the person from the context of the conversation.

In addition Wittgenstein is entirely unclear and vague about whatever a person perceives to be the meaning of something verbal that the person either hears or reads.

What is lacking in Wittgenstein's and other common philosophical notions about language is a clear understanding of the relation between a person's perception of something linguistic and the person's perception of all other kinds of impressions. There is talk about the linguistic activity without a clear understanding of its relation to the person's *stream of thought*. Thereby it is lost from sight that a person's perception of something linguistic does not in any essential way differ from the person's perception of any other impressions.

For example when I see before me an oblong yellow thing, which has one end formed into a point, and thereby perceive that there is a pencil lying on my table, this is not essentially different from my seeing a pattern of black ink drawn on a sheet of paper before me, thus: 'Partitur', and thereby perceiving that the text that follows on the paper talks about what is in Danish called a 'partitur', in English a musical score. In both cases that which I see, by *association* in my stream of thought calls forth another *thought object* in the steam (see *stream of thought*).

When I see the oblong yellow thing, a thought object is called forth in my stream of thought, which for lack of anything better may be denoted pencil. But this denotation is entirely insufficient for describing the object of my thought. In this object is found, centrally, the thought about the writing tool, with its lead of graphite and its envelope of wood. Centrally is found also my feelings about this particular pencil, positive feelings about the convenience of the pencil in the use I have made of it in making notes. More peripherally in the object of my thought, in what is called the fringe of the object, there are vague suggestions of thoughts of other pencils I have had and used, of various denotations that may be applied, such as blyant, bleistift, crayon, of the pocket in my shirt in which I sometimes carry pencils, and of the special gatherings in the summer at which I often carry small pencils in this way. And so on, in many directions, with countless other vague connections of thoughts and feelings. *All this as one whole*—and more besides—is the meaning coming forth in my stream of thought when I see the yellow thing.

When I read the word 'Partitur', as written on a sheet of paper before me this moment, an object in my stream of thought comes forth in a like manner. This object has at its center thoughts about the notes concerning my work on scores that I have recorded on the paper. The scores here denoted by the word are such that I intend to work out in the time to come. Thus at this moment they exist merely as images in my stream of thought. In addition the object has feelings of my vivid interest in my work with scores. In its fringe the object has vague thoughts about the works of music that I have already worked out as scores, about other works that I would like to work out, about the challenges and problems that arise from such work, about the musical activity that may be initiated by a score, and much more. *All this as one whole*—and more besides—is the meaning coming forth in my stream of thought when at this moment I see the word 'Partitur', as it is written on a sheet of paper.

But now I change my view and see the text 'Partitura d'Orchestra', as it appears in golden letters on a thick book with a greenish cover lying on my table. This text immediately by association calls forth a new object in my steam of thought. This object in its core has the thought of the score of Verdi's opera Otello that lies before me, with its many pages of notes that express Verdi's music. To this core is attached in my thought strong positive feelings of joy over this marvellous work and admiration for the great master who has created it. In its fringe the objects has a lot of purely musical thoughts, of the sound of melodies from the work and of voices that I have heard singing them, in addition to thoughts about Shakespeare's absorbing drama, of the terrible Jago, the tortured Otello, and the poor mishandled Desdemona. *All this as one whole*—and more besides—is the meaning coming forth in my stream of thought when I see the word 'Partitura', as it is printed in gold on a thick book upon my table.

And if by chance the same thick book had been lying with the back side up, so that I would catch sight of the green cover, but without letters, then the thought the book would call forth in me would be just the same. Thus the perception of something verbal is not different, psychologically, from any other *perception* (q.v.).

The sound produced when something is pushed through the mail slit in the front door of my house calls forth in me roughly the same thought object as would a person saying to me: 'The postman has just been here'.

The objects that are thus by *association* called forth in my stream of thought, depend upon my *dispositions*, as they have been trained during a long life (see *habit*).

But now Wittgenstein and other philosophers insist that the word 'partitur' has a meaning, independently of any context. These people have not understood anything about how language and thought activity works. And they get no help to a better understanding from the present day psychologists. These are committed to *behaviorism*. This builds upon the science philosophers' claim that science is a matter of truth. Thus the psychologists cannot allow themselves to talk about what I experience, the thoughts and feelings that fill my stream of thought, because they cannot be seen on my outside and be checked whether they are what I say. So when I say that my feelings are so and so and influence my actions in such and such a manner, the present day psychologist will not listen to me.

Further references are given in the Literature Appendix.

Language of science: The phrase 'the language of science' enters into the philosophers' explanations of certain *–isms*, and Einstein has a short essay under that title. In the very phrase there is much misleading unclarity. Not only the unclarity that comes from any talk of a language as something definite, something delimited (see *word-as-code-of-meaning-fallacy, language-as-something-fallacy*). But additionally the implicit claim that the mythical preacher called science should employ a definite, special language.

The matters that lie behind these misleading manners of speaking may be clarified briefly in the following manner. Every scientific activity seeks to form descriptions of some aspect of the world (see *scientific-scholarly activity*). Any description makes use of elements of description of some kind or other. Usually a mixture of descriptive elements is used. These may be words taken from daily life, they may be words invented for the purpose, they may be figures of a certain kind, they may be tables, or items taken from mathematics, such as numbers and functions, or they may be computational process descriptions, physical models, and many other things. An important part of the scientific activity is to *choose the description form* (q.v.) of whatever is described. A fortunate choice of description form may lead to a scientific break-through. Example: Newton's description of motion in terms of velocities and accelerations.

Thus every scientific contribution makes use of one or several definite forms of description. Some like to say that it is expressed in a particular scientific language. But this is a misleading, harmful manner of speaking. Misleading by suggesting that it makes sense to talk of *one* language, of something definite. Harmful by suggesting that different scientific contributions ought to use the same description form.

Language philosophy: Linguistics and philosophy, whatever they are, get along in a problematic and unclear symbiosis. Part of the problem has been characterized strikingly by Ryle in an article: *Systematically Misleading Expressions* from 1932:

'Philosophical arguments have always largely, if not entirely, consisted in attempts to thrash out "what it means to say so and so". It is observed that men in their ordinary discourse, the discourse, that is, that they employ when they are not philosophizing, use certain expressions, and philosophers fasten on to certain more or less radical types or classes of such expressions and raise their question about all expressions of a certain type and ask what they really mean.

Sometimes philosophers say that they are analysing or clarifying the "concepts" which are embodied in the "judgements" of the plain man or of the scientist, historian, artist, or who-not. But this seems to be only a gaseous way of saying that they are trying to discover what is meant by the general terms contained in the sentences which they pronounce or write. For, as we shall see, "*x* is a concept" and "*y* is a judgement" are themselves systematically misleading expressions.

But the whole procedure is very odd. For, if the expressions under consideration are intelligently used, their employers must already know what they mean and do not need the aid or admonition of philosophers before they can understand what they are saying.

And if their hearers understand what they are being told, they too are in no such perplexity that they need to have this meaning philosophically "analyzed" or "clarified" for them. And, at least, the philosopher himself must know what the expressions mean, since otherwise he could not know what it was that he was analysing.'

In view of this pronouncement from Ryle it is immediately surprising that his best known contribution, the book *The Concept of Mind*, at first sight seems to be concerned precisely with what our sayings mean. The point is that this first sight is misleading, however. Viewed more closely, what Ryle has done in his book is to investigate how certain characteristics of human thinking can be derived from the locutions that are meaningfully applied to human beings. Thus Ryle does *not* ask what certain expressions mean. Instead he takes carefully selected, ordinary locutions and investigates what they tell about how we may describe human mental life. Like Austin, Ryle builds his discussion upon his own introspective feeling about the meaningfulness of certain locutions. For an example, see *knowing*. On Ryle's book see also *logic*.

Further references are given in the Literature Appendix.

Language-as-something-fallacy: This is the notion that linguistic phenomena may be described as properties of specific languages, for example English or Danish, each of which is supposed to be clearly delimited. The fallacy is closely related to the *word-as-code-of-meaning-fallacy,* q.v.

The language-as-something-fallacy finds expression in titles such as *Dictionary of the American Language*, by the use of the phrase 'the American Language' in definite form. Another expression of the fallacy is the phrase 'the logic of language', which is composed of two words, 'logic' and 'language', neither of which denotes anything specific. 'The logic of language' and 'the rules that the language itself is based upon' are favourite nonsense phrases of present day philosophers (see for example pronouncements by Kjørup, Favrholdt, Collin, and Zinkernagel, quoted in Weekendavisen for 1998 January 1, and by Ryle, quoted in the article about *logic*). These phrases have become popular after 'the existence of God' went out of fashion in philosophy.

An alternative to the language-as-something-fallacy is to conceive language as a matter of certain human habits. This is the notion we find in the writings of Otto Jespersen and William James, see *word-as-code-of-meaning-fallacy*. With this notion language is tied to individual persons. Because of the plenitude of the linguistic habits, both in the single individual and even more in the individuals forming a society, and because the habits are in incessant change, it is entirely impracticable to describe language in its fullness.

The speech habits of an individual or a community of persons can only be described incompletely as those features of the habits that retain a certain permanence and that are shared by all the members of the community. These features are most prominently the spoken and written words that enter into the habits. The associations of understanding that are called forth by the words in the individual person also depend upon all kinds of additional circumstances in the state of mind of the person, and so are manifold beyond any description. Descriptions by necessity have to be limited to indicating certain common features of the understanding usually called forth in the individuals of a certain linguistic community at a certain period. Dictionaries and grammars are catalogs of such descriptions.

Each person in his or her intercourse with his or her fellow beings normally makes use of a series of speech styles, each style having developed itself within a certain circle of persons. These speech styles cannot be distinguished sharply from other modes of expression that are employed in the gatherings of each circle.

See also *concept, logic, language of science.*

Language-fallacy: A significant part of the philosophical inanity is closely related to fallacious notions about the human linguistic activity. These fallacies form a connected net, which has here been split into separate items: *concept-is-word-fallacy, language-as-something-fallacy, language-rule-fallacy, thinking-as-language-fallacy, understand-fallacy, word-as-code-of-meaning-fallacy,* qq.v.

Language-rule-fallacy: This fallacy has been expressed, for example, by Einstein in *The Common Language of Science*: 'If language is to lead at all to understanding, there must be rules concerning the relations between the signs on the one hand and on the other hand there must a stable correspondence between signs and impressions.' That the fallacy lies close at hand is apparent from the fact that even Otto Jespersen occasionally falls into its trap. Even though on page 16 of *Essentials of English Grammar* he has stressed that 'Language is nothing but a set of human habits ...', he on page 20 talks about '... the rules followed instinctively by speakers and writers.' But this last phrase is misleading; *to act from habit is not to follow a rule* (see *know-how*).

Philosophical discussion around language rules has in recent years been presented prominently by Chomsky. He is interested in language rules of the type called generative grammar. A rule of generative grammar tells how linguistic elements may be put together, such that sentences may be composed of the individual words that enter into them. According to Chomsky all linguistic activity consists in processes taking place in the person, such that the rules of a generative grammar are used. Chomsky says that every person possesses the rules of a generative grammar of his language.

The fallacy of Chomsky's talk about language rules is displayed prominently when he writes (*Language and Mind*, p. 115):

'It is quite obvious that sentences have an intrinsic meaning determined by linguistic rule and that a person with command of a language has in some way internalized the system of rules that determine both the phonetic shape of the sentence and its intrinsic semantic content—that he has developed what we will refer to as a specific *linguistic competence*. However, it is equally clear that the actual observed use of language—actual *performance*—does not simply reflect the intrinsic sound-meaning connections established by the system of linguistic rules. Performance involves many other factors as well. We do not interpret what is said in our presence simply by application of the *linguistic* principles that determine the phonetic and semantic properties of an utterance. Extralinguistic beliefs concerning the speaker and the situation play a fundamental role in determining how speech is produced, identified, and understood.'

Language-rule-fallacy ...

In this passage Chomsky has served us by presenting the language-rule-fallacy in a nutshell. As a matter of fact, the passage is one big contradiction of itself. In the first sentence it is maintained as 'quite obvious' that 'sentences have an intrinsic meaning determined by linguistic rule', and the last sentence: 'Extralinguistic beliefs ...', is a direct contradiction of the first one. The talk about 'specific *linguistic competence*' is empty twaddle, philosophical mist. The passage is thick of foggy and meaningless denotations: 'person with command of a language', 'the sentence and its intrinsic semantic content'. The talk about 'intrinsic meaning' is pure Aristotelian philosophical nonsense.

This inanity of Chomsky's presentation may be illustrated by a closer consideration of his own examples of how a person's linguistic understanding should involve the person's use of rules for transforming the utterances. More particularly, Chomsky maintains that the understanding depends on the formation of a so-called deep structure of what is directly heard or read. But ordinary people, as we all know, are not aware of rules and deep structures for their utterances. Thus Chomsky has to postulate that every linguistic activity depends on a transformation of the utterances according to complicated rules taking place in some unknown place.

Let us in order to illustrate Chomsky's ideas take one of his examples of how linguistic understanding supposedly depends upon structure rules. The example is:

'They don't know how good meat tastes.'

This sentence may in suitable contexts be understood in two manners. According to manner 1 it is said that certain persons ('they') do not know the taste of good meat. According to manner 2 it is said that certain persons do not know how good the taste of meat is. Chomsky now maintains that distinguishing between the two manners is conditioned upon an analysis of the sentence with the aid of structure rules, in such a way that it is shown in structure diagrams that 'good' in manner 1 qualifies 'meat', while 'good' in manner 2 qualifies 'tastes'.

But Chomsky's insistence that language rules are necessary for the understanding of the given sentence lacks reasonable justification. The point is that the two manners may be distinguished merely from the way the words are habitually understood, corresponding to how they are explained in a dictionary. It is a matter of the word 'good'. As anybody knows one may in ordinary English style talk of 'good meat', as well as of that 'something tastes good'. It so happens that the English sentence fails to make clear which of these two uses of 'good' the speaker has had in mind. The speaker has expressed himself unclearly.

The understanding of the ambiguity of the sentence may thus be described as a result of the person's habitual associations between thoughts and words, like any other linguistic understanding.

Still more revealing of Chomsky's misconceptions is his talk of the child's language acquisition. He writes (*Language and Mind,* p. 158):

'The child must acquire a generative grammar of his language on the basis of a fairly restricted amount of evidence. *Footnote:* Furthermore, evidence of a highly degraded sort. For example, the child's conclusions about the rules of sentence formation must be based on evidence that consists, to a large extent, of utterances that break rules, since a good deal of normal speech consists of false starts, disconnected phrases, and other deviations from idealized competence.'

The inanity of this understanding of a child's language acquisition is clear as soon as one considers the assumption behind: that a person's understanding of each linguistic signal depends on the person's use of the rules of a generative grammar. But the newborn child has not acquired Chomsky's rules, and thus by the assumption is unable to understand *any* linguistic signal. In particular the child is barred from conceiving certain of these signals as evidence of rules. The acquisition process postulated by Chomsky is impossible.

On the basis of such incoherent nonsense Chomsky philosophizes pages full about what we may derive from generative grammars about the innate properties of people.

The language philosophers' talk of rules that are used every time we say something and every time we hear something said by others is weird from any point of view. If one asks ordinary people about what rules they use when they talk together one will get no clear answer. But, the philosopher will say, these rules work in 'the unconsciousness' (see *consciousness*), therefore people don't know them. We are thus supposed to understand our conversation activity to be controlled by hidden rules.

But what do these hidden language rules say? Think of the situation described in the article about the *word-as-code-of-meaning-fallacy*. Which hidden rules have been in use when the person mentioned there said to his lunch companion 'Will you pass me the bread, please'? Which rules decided that the person started by saying 'Will you ...'?

A rule has to be a kind of machine, that each time it is put to action by an impulse of a certain kind delivers something specific, like a drink automat, which in dependence upon the button one has pressed will deliver coffee, juice, or cola. Is there a hidden language rule of this type: When one want to ask for something one must start by saying 'Will you ...'?

But this the rule cannot say, since the person might also have started his request by saying: 'May I bother you ...', or 'If you don't mind, will you ...', or 'Will my companion have the grace to ...', or yet another of numerous possible phrases. The rule has to be more elaborate. It must include factors that enter into selecting among such possibilities. But the choice between for example 'Will you ...' and 'May I bother you ...' cannot be described by such criteria that might enter into releasing a rule, it is an expression of a personal, situation-dependent mood. It it simply not possible to extract sharp criteria of that in the situation that leads to the linguistic expression actually produced; that expression is a result of the person's whole mental state at the moment of speaking.

Furthermore, even if such a hidden language rule were there, a decisive question remains: How does it happen that *precisely this rule goes into action*, and not one of the thousands of others? What decides the choice of rule? This is not answered by the philosophers.

If we want to arrive at a tenable understanding of language rules we need only look at the rules that may be found in grammars. We will then soon find that these rules are not of such a form that they might specify something about the meaning of linguistic utterances. The rules are *descriptive of the habits of certain writers*, but useless as guide to finding a text that expresses a given thought. The habits described have been gleaned from texts selected by the grammarian, typically literary novelistic style.

Language-rule-fallacy ...

Instead of the philosophical fallacies about language rules one may put:

(1) Language rules are *descriptive* of a certain language style.

(2) Language rules may be useful to a speaker or writer who wishes to express himself or herself in a style he or she does not have as a habit.

(3) Language rules may be a help to a school master who wishes to indicate that a speaker or writer either does not wish or is unable to express himself or herself in a certain style.

See also *grammar*. Further references are given in the Literature Appendix.

Law of nature: 'Law of nature' is a misleading denotation for a *description* (q.v.) that covers a certain class of aspects of the world. See *physics, philosophy of science, Popper*. Further references are given in the Literature Appendix.

Leibniz, Gottfried Wilhelm: See *mathematical analysis*.

Linguistic meaning: See *word-as-code-of-meaning-fallacy*.

Locke, John: See *association, psychology*.

Logic: Logic! is the war cry of the philosophical presumption. Philosophers' talk of logic extends far and wide, but with the common feature that logic, even if it is quite unclear what is meant thereby, to a philosopher it is something wholesome that he masters, something that helps him along the road to the truth that his heart is yearning for.

This feeling about the word 'logic' is shared far outside the circle of philosophers, not the least among academics. Typically the school masters say that the pupils must learn to think logically, with the understanding that so they do themselves. Characteristically this very manner of speaking is pure nonsense. Thinking is not something somebody does in one way or another, it is something that goes on, see *stream of thought*.

As illustration of the philosophical talk about logic some examples taken from philosophers' texts are discussed below. Further examples may be found under *mathematical logic*.

Aristotle uses the word logic about *linguistic statements* that by their form suggest that they are either right or wrong, true or false, and about *proofs* that they are one or the other. The classical example is:

Every Greek is a man.
Every man is mortal.
Every Greek is mortal.

These three lines are called a logical proof. The first two lines of the proof are called the premises, which in the context of the proof are considered to be true. By the proof we allegedly get access to a new truth, the conclusion, which in the example is that every Greek is mortal. This truth is said to be 'derived logically' from the premises. It is also said that thereby a 'logical inference' has been made. The word logic in this case denotes a certain structure of some linguistic statements.

The example has a certain plausibility. This is the kind of thing which is presented in school to the children, who are then expected to be suitably impressed. Perhaps they are, the innocent young. But the matter reveals itself at closer consideration to be full of problems that the school masters say nothing about.

In the first place one may consider the use in the premises of the words 'every' and 'is'. The two phrases 'every Greek' and 'every man', what do they denote? What do these sentences talk about? Both Greeks and men come and disappear, are born and die. There come steadily new, day after day. Who can pronounce truths about them? Even a property that has been found to hold for all Greeks who have lived until today may be found not to hold for a Greek who is born tomorrow. How can a philosopher, who yearns to tell what is correct, allow himself to pronounce a property of every Greek, or every man?

Next consider the use of 'is' in the proof. How is this word to be understood here? 'Is' is the most ambiguous word there is, see *is*.

An example as problematic as this is revealing of the mystique of logic. Used as illustration of logic in the elementary education the example exercises linguistic expressions containing descriptive phrases lacking a clear reference, in other words the example trains the acceptance of nonsense without protest. The sensible reaction to the school master's talk of 'every Greek' would be the protest: What is he talking about? Why does he talk nonsense? But this reaction would not be popular with the presumptuous school master, as the children are perfectly aware.

As further illustration of the philosophers' way of talking about logic we shall here reproduce what we find in Bertrand Russell's *The Analysis of Mind*. This source is of special interest since Russell was the leading logician of his time. His book was reprinted 11 times during the years 1921 to 1978. Surprisingly the book does not take up logic for special treatment and the word logic is found in the book only in four contexts, the first on page 112:

'Our perception is made up of sensations, images and beliefs, but the supposed "object" is something inferential, externally related, not logically bound up with what is occurring in us.'

A more helplessly nonsensical pronouncement about our mental life is hard to imagine. Russell evidently does not connect anything clearly with sensations, images, and beliefs, and their mutual relations. And what might be the meaning of 'logically bound up with what is occurring in us'? Misty talk!

On p. 158 of Russell's book we find:

'Why do we believe that images are, sometimes or always, approximately or exactly, copies of sensations? What sort of evidence is there? And what sort of evidence is logically possible?'

To such nonsensical questions only one kind of answer is conceivable: further nonsense. On p. 159:

'It is not logically necessary to the existence of a memory-belief that the event remembered should have occurred, or even that the past should have existed at all. There is no logical impossibility in the hypothesis that the world sprang into being five minutes ago, exactly as it then was, with a population that 'remembered' a wholly unreal past. There is no logically necessary connection between events at different times; therefore nothing that is happening now or will happen in the future can disprove the hypothesis that the world began five minutes ago. Hence the occurrences which are *called* knowledge of the past are logically independent of the past.'

Logic ...

From this pronouncement by the great expert in logic the only lesson to be derived is that what he calls logic does not contribute to our understanding of the ways of the world. Finally on p. 195:

'There is no *logical* impossibility in walking occurring as an isolated phenomenon, not forming part of any such series as we call a "person".'

From this may be inferred that in clarifying ordinary locutions, logic is powerless.

The most positive one may say about these examples from Russell's book is that they provide striking demonstrations of the worthlessness of logic for our understanding. If logic has no more to offer than these sorts of things we may safely leave it to the philosophers' continued twaddle.

As yet another illustration of the philosophers' use of the word logic we shall look more closely at certain passages in Gilbert Ryle's *The Concept of Mind*. In the Introduction, on p. 10, Ryle writes:

'For certain purposes it is necessary to determine the logical crossbearings of the concepts which we know quite well how to apply. ... it is part of the thesis of this book that during the three centuries of the epoch of natural science the logical categories in terms of which the concepts of mental powers and operations have been coordinated have been wrongly selected. ...

To determine the logical geography of concepts is to reveal the logic of the propositions in which they are wielded, that is to say, to show with what other propositions they are consistent and inconsistent, what propositions follow from them and from what propositions they follow. The logical type or category to which a concept belongs is the set of ways in which it is logically legitimate to operate with it. The key arguments employed in this book are therefore intended to show why certain sorts of operations with the concepts of mental powers and processes are breaches of logical rules. I try to use *reductio ad absurdum* arguments ...'

This passage shows how Ryle expressly solicits logic in support of his argumentation. In the closer examination below the passage is found to be a network of unclear formulations. In addition, it is misleading in relation to the way Ryle argues later in his book.

The unclarity of the passage is in the first place related to the talk of concepts and logical categories. It talks first of 'the concepts which we know quite well how to apply'. But in the next sentence the subject is 'the logical categories in terms of which the concepts of mental powers and operations have been coordinated'. Already here one may feel uncertain. One may ask oneself, are 'the concepts of mental powers and operations' given beforehand, without connection with logical categories? If so, how? And what are logical categories? Do they differ from categories, and if so how? And what does it mean that 'concepts ... have been coordinated'?

The statement 'To determine the logical geography of concepts is to reveal the logic of the propositions in which they are wielded' involves far-reaching and problematic assumptions. Thus the statement must presuppose that concepts are wielded in propositions, and additionally that 'propositions in which they are wielded' are given beforehand. Building upon such misty matters as 'the logic of the propositions in which they are wielded', the formulation is a typical philosopher's pronouncement. This unclear talk of concepts and propositions is an expression of the *concept-is-word-fallacy*, q.v.

Ryle's talk of logic is most explicit where he says: 'The logical type or category to which a concept belongs is the set of ways in which it is logically legitimate to operate with it. ... certain sorts of operations with the concepts of mental powers and processes are breaches of logical rules.' This sounds very impressive, but at closer look appears as a swamp of unclarity. What does it mean: 'way of operating with a concept'? How do we know, Ryle or the reader, what is 'logically legitimate'? What are the logical rules Ryle talks about, and where do they come from?

But the matter gets closer to a clarification if we consider Ryle's first statement: '... the logical categories in terms of which the concepts of mental powers and operations have been coordinated have been wrongly selected'. In this statement it is implied that what Ryle maintains first of all is that *certain logical categories have been wrongly selected*. The subsequent talk of logic and rules is merely an additional claim: the wrongness is a matter of logic.

In order to clarify the matter further we must look at some examples of how Ryle argues explicitly with what he calls logic. Thus on pp. 112-13 of his book we find:

'Chapter V - Dispositions and Occurrences
(1) *Foreword*
    I have already had occasion to argue that a number of the words which we commonly use to describe and explain people's behaviour signify dispositions and not episodes. To say that a person knows something, or aspires to be something, is not to say that he is at a particular moment in process of doing or undergoing anything, but that he is able to do certain things, when the need arises, or that he is prone to do and feel certain things in situations of certain sorts.
    This is, in itself, hardly more than a dull fact (almost) of ordinary grammar. The verbs "know", "possess", and "aspire" do not behave like the verbs "run", "wake up", or "tingle"; we cannot say "he knew so and so for two minutes, then stopped and started again after a breather", "he gradually aspired to be a bishop, or "he is now engaged in possessing a bicycle". Nor is it a peculiarity of people that we describe them in dispositional terms. We use such terms just as much for describing animals, insects, crystals, and atoms....
(2) *The Logic of Dispositional Statements*
    When a cow is said to be a ruminant, or a man is said to be a cigarette-smoker, it is not being said that the cow is ruminating now or that the man is smoking a cigarette now. To be a ruminant is to tend to ruminate from time to time, and to be a cigarette-smoker is to be in the habit of smoking cigarettes. ... "He is smoking a cigarette now" does not say the same sort of thing as "he is a cigarette-smoker", but unless statements like the first were sometimes true, statements like the second could not be true.'

Like the Introduction to the book these passages consist of an opaque mixture of valuable insight and philosophical muddle. A valuable clarification is contributed when Ryle in the first sentence of the chapter uses the phrase 'the words which we commonly use to describe and explain people's behaviour'. This phrase shows first that the center of Ryle's interest here is *description of people's behaviour*.

Second, speaking in this context of 'the words which we commonly use' indicates that Ryle intends to build his argumentation upon *the linguistic habits in the society in which he belongs.*

But the matter is immediately philosophically muddled when Ryle continues to say: 'This is, in itself, hardly more than a dull fact (almost) of ordinary grammar. The verbs "know" ... do not behave like the verbs "run" ...'. With these words Ryle implies that there are facts of ordinary grammar that are not merely descriptions of the linguistic habits in a society, and that the words 'know', 'run', etc. have an independent life, such that they are able to 'behave'.

The muddle in this becomes evident as soon as we are so impolite as to enquire into the source of the alleged 'facts ... of ordinary grammar'. Consulting Jespersen's *Essentials of English Grammar* does not help, it tells nothing about these aspects of meaning. The explanation of the word 'smoker' in Webster's Dictionary: 'One who or that which smokes', does not clarify the use of the word as description of a personal disposition. Ryle's talk of 'facts ... of ordinary grammar' shows him to be committed to the *language-as-something-fallacy*, q.v.

The insight into human characteristics that Ryle derives from the ordinary locutions is not something Ryle or anybody else has acquired through a study of grammar books, or derived by rules of logic; they are generally known by anyone who *habitually masters the relevant locutions.* The philosophers' 'facts of grammar' or logic, whatever they are, contribute nothing further.

A similar mixture of valuable insight and philosophical muddle is found in the section about 'The Logic of Dispositional Statements'. The valuable contribution is that Ryle turns the attention to the understanding that in relevant linguistic communities is expressed by such statements as 'P is a ruminant', 'Q ruminates', 'R is a cigarette-smoker', and 'S is smoking a cigarette now', and thereby opens to the *description of human dispositions* that may be derived from a comprehensive class of locutions. But the talk of the truths of statements and their mutual relations are insignificant details. The talk of logic that supposedly determines the understanding of 'P is a ruminant' etc. is merely philosophical nonsense.

Thus this chapter in Ryle's book brings an insight into properties of human beings that are inherent in *the ordinary understanding of the locutions that habitually are used to describe and explain human behavior.* The common use in the community of these descriptive statements is evidence that the members of this community understand and acknowledge that human beings have habits, dispositions, of many different kinds.

For Ryle's argumentation as a whole it holds that it builds upon ordinary *introspective understanding of linguistic habits.* The talk of logic in this context merely contributes philosophical confusion.

In summary, the word 'logic' has been used in philosophical gibberish to such an extent that it is useless in sensible talk.

Further references are given in the Literature Appendix.

Mathematical analysis: Mathematical analysis, which comprises differential and integral calculus, is next to numbers and computing the most important part of mathematics. Unlike numbers and computing, mathematical analysis originated in historical times, invented by Newton og Leibniz. But philosophers do not know much about it. They prefer to talk of logic, as Aristotle did. *Dictionary of Philosophy* has four lines about mathematical analysis, half a page about numbers, and 11 pages about logic.

This disproportion is related to the fact that mathematical analysis deals with description forms that are suitable for continuously varying items, such as time, distance, electrical fields, and many others. Such descriptions are obviously enormously more useful than descriptions that only care for what may be said in terms of yes/no, or true/false. Practically all modern technology, both building, electronics, and space travel, builds upon mathematical analytic descriptions. What may be described in terms of logic is very little in comparison.

But to the philosopher, in his Aristotelian fixation, all this mathematical analysis has no interest, because it does not talk about anything that is true or false. The mathematical analytic descriptions are difficult to establish, they demand mastery of a large arsenal of techniques of mathematics and computing. Part of the difficulty is that a mathematical analytic description only in very few special cases may be worked out exactly. In by far the most cases the mathematician has to simplify his problem by introducing approximations in the mathematical description. Thus all such descriptions aim merely at finding approximations to what may be measured about how the world behaves. And again the descriptions never fit perfectly. Whether they would fit if they might be worked out exactly, no one can say.

All this is partly incomprehensible, partly irritating to philosophers, and for several hundred years the physicists and astronomers have been able very successfully to develop their mathematical analytic descriptions without interference from the philosophers. But from the middle of the nineteenth century the philosophers have again been meddling with such questions as: Which theories are true? Is mathematics true? For more of this see *foundations, philosophy of science*.

See also *scientific-scholarly activity*. Further references are given in the Literature Appendix.

Mathematical logic: 'Mathematical logic' is a mantra for present day philosophers. In a report in Weekendavisen 1. Jan. 1998 both Collin and Zinkernagel mention mathematical and formal logic as something quite special, as part of what they call objective knowledge.

Significantly, mathematical logic was first suggested by Boole in 1857 in a paper with the title *The Laws of Thought*. By putting this title on his paper Boole reveals a total miscomprehension of the activity of human thinking. Boole's contribution is merely to denote the words 'and' and 'or' in certain of their ordinary uses by special symbols. This idea is so simple and trivial that even philosophers can grasp it. But that thereby something about human thinking has been said, one has to be philosopher to maintain.

Mathematical logic was launched first of all by Bertrand Russell and A. N. Whitehead. Their thick *Principia Mathematica* was published around 1910. Principia Mathematica is a classic of mathematics of the kind that everybody talks about and nobody reads. It has hundreds of pages of formulas in a symbolism that was invented by the authors for the purpose. With these formulas it is shown how mathematics through formalized logical proofs may be developed from the theory of sets.

Mathematical logic ...

The endeavour that unfolds in Principia Mathematica is peculiar in several ways. The program is centered around the mathematics that for centuries has been found perfectly useful for descriptions in many different contexts, in trade, in traffic, in building, in astronomy, etc. The program aims at giving a *proof* that all this mathematics is *true* (see *truth*). But what is to be understood as such a proof is by no means given in advance. In order that the problem is to make sense it is necessary to *decide* what such a proof is like. The two authors of Principia Mathematica have decided to start from a few statements, so-called *axioms, that are assumed to be true*, together with certain *rules of inference* that make it possible to derive new true statements from such true statements that are already at hand. These new statements are then said to be *proven* to be true.

Already this main line is peculiar. The endeavour aims at proving that something is true, but the first thing done is to assume, *choose* the axioms and the rules of inference. These are as pulled out of a hat. Why do they have to be accepted as true? Because from them Russell and Whitehead are able to prove such properties of well known mathematical subjects, for example numbers, that already for ages have been ascertained and have been useful in applications. Thus the whole activity is a formal game, in which certain pieces may be moved according to certain rules. It will appeal to anyone with a taste for formal games, since it unfolds in Principia Mathematica with formulas, page after page, hundreds of them. Thus on page 345 the number 1 is defined, and on page 357 the number 2. The definitions look like this:

*52.01 $1 = \hat{\alpha}\left\{(\exists x).\alpha = \iota'x\right\}$ Df

*54.02 $2 = \hat{\alpha}\left\{(\exists x,y).x \neq y.\alpha = \iota'x \cup \iota'y\right\}$ Df

Russell himself was well satisfied with this way to define the numbers. In his *Introduction to Mathematical Philosophy* from 1919 he says on p. 18:

> 'We naturally think that the class of couples (for example) is something different from the number 2. But there is no doubt about the class of couples: it is indubitable and not difficult to define, whereas the number 2, in any other sense, is a metaphysical entity about which we can never feel sure that it exists or that we have tracked it down. It is therefore more prudent to content ourselves with the class of couples, which we are sure of, than to hunt for a problematic number 2 which must always remain elusive.'

Russell's way of expressing himself here is significant. He dismisses any other meaning of the number 2 saying that we cannot feel sure about it. In saying so Russell admits the *feeling of certainty* which in his thought comes with a mathematical definition, as a decisive circumstance for mathematical logic.

But *whose* feeling of certainty is to be decisive here? Russell's, or yours, or mine? Talking only of what I know of, I can say that my feeling is quite different from Russell's. I do not at all feel sure about the class of pairs. Try to consider what lies in these words: the class of pairs. It has to be the collection of anything that may be called pairs, all pairs that have been, all that are there today, and all that will come until—until when? Pairs of all conceivable kinds, shoes, seagulls, violin tones, gushes of air, clouds, etc. etc. This thought of the class of pairs to me fades into vague uncertainty.

Do I have anything to put instead of it? Certainly, the numbers, as every child knows, are one, two, three, etc. Put slightly differently it is a single series of successors. Each number has one definite successor. Then we may start from either one or zero, as we like. Thus the numbers, in my understanding, are something we have to imagine each of us, to wit a series of imagined things of some kind, that are all different but form a single chain. When we use the numbers, for example for counting a number of particular things, we in our thought attach some of the numbers to the thought of the individual things. This way to understand the numbers corresponds to *Peano's axioms.*

The way the mathematical logic is grounded in personal feelings may at closer look be seen to have far wider significance. In fact, Russell and Whitehead's choice of the theory of sets as the starting point of their axioms is entirely a matter of their personal feelings. Russell and Whitehead chose the theory of sets because they *felt* that therein they had a *reliable* tool, a tool that by its simplicity would ensure them against false inferences. But in this they were seriously mistaken. Contrary to their expectation Russell in the middle of their great work on Principia Mathematica discovered that their basic tool, the theory of sets, admitted the introduction of contradictions into their description of mathematics. Russell himself discovered a type of contradiction, thereafter called Russell's paradox. The issue is that there are easy means of defining new sets of all kinds. But it turns out that one may get into trouble when defining such sets. It is in fact possible, with a bit of cleverness, to define a set having properties that are not clearly defined. This corresponds to talking about a thing that is both red and not red.

The discovery of the paradox was a shock to Russell. The theory of sets, which he had thought to be an unfailingly reliable tool, was flawed. He did not abandon his project, however, but engaged into a repair operation, which was called the theory of types of set theory. In this way his whole project got to be far more opaque. Who will believe that these hundreds of unreadable pages have no errors in them? Perhaps they have even more deep flaws than the paradoxes.

The later development in mathematics has only confirmed the problematic and uncertain character of mathematical logic. The mathematicians could not agree what to consider a valid proof. Several sects sprang up, each having its adherents. A famous event happened in 1930 when Gödel gave a proof that a certain procedure for constructing a so-called logical foundation never will be able to justify the mathematics which is actually used. This development shows that truth in mathematics in the last resort is a matter of a personal *feeling*. It confirms William James's account of *reality*, q.v.

And what insight into people and their thinking comes out of all this trouble, all these pages of unreadable formulas? Of this it is most natural to let Russell himself speak, so let us examine his book *The Analysis of Mind* from 1921. Here we meet the surprise that the book has no special discussion of logic; no chapter heading mentions logic and the word logic does not appear in the index. There remain only a few passages where the word logic or logical appears explicitly, see *logic*. Mathematical logic is mentioned by Russell only on p. 88:

'Believers in psycho-physical parallelism … believe that every psychical event has a psychical cause and a physical concomitant. If there is to be parallelism, it is easy to prove by mathematical logic that the causation in physical and psychical matters must be of the same sort, and it is impossible that mnemic causation should exist in psychology but not in physics.'

Mathematical logic ...

This is a curious statement, particularly when written by Russell. He has himself in detail shown how the philosophical talk about causes is nonsense (see *cause*). The sense of 'causation in physical and psychical matters must be of the same sort' is shrouded in a mist, which is not made less dense with the talk of mathematical logic.

See also *philosophy of science*. Further references are given in the Literature Appendix.

Matter: The word enters in the philosophers' explanations of certain –*isms*. What it denotes outside of any context no one can tell. See also *reality*.

Mental object: See *stream of thought*.

Mentalism: *Dictionary of Philosophy* explains mentalism thus: 'Metaphysical theory of the exclusive reality of individual minds and their subjective states.' This is empty talk since 'reality' outside of any context denotes nothing. See –*ism, reality*.

Metaphysics: See *is*.

Meteorology: See *philosophy of science*.

Mill, John Stuart: See *association, cause, philosophy of science*.

Mind: The word mind is occasionally used to denote the *stream of thought*.

Model: The word model is used in for example physics and astronomy to denote a form of description. A prominent example is Niels Bohr's model of the hydrogen atom from 1913. See *description*. Further references are given in the Literature Appendix.

Monism: *Dictionary of Philosophy* explains monism thus: '(a) Metaphysical: The view that there is but one fundamental Reality. (b) Epistemological: The view that the real object and the idea of it (perception or conception) are one in the knowledge relation.' These explanations say nothing since it is unclear what in the context is meant by 'Reality', 'the real object', and 'the knowledge relation'.

Moon, theory of: See *cause*.

Nativism: Nativism is defined in *Dictionary of Philosophy* as 'Theory that mind has elements of knowledge not derived from sensation.' This is unclear by the talk of 'elements of knowledge', see *knowledge*. See also –*ism*.

Necessity: The word necessity enters into the philosophers' explanations of certain –*isms*. *Dictionary of Philosophy* says: 'A state of affairs is said to be necessary if it cannot be otherwise than it is.' This explanation builds upon the Aristotelian-philosophical *is* (q.v.) and shares its unclarity. See also *cause*.

Newton, Isaac: See *cause, language of science, mathematical analysis, Newtonian mechanics*.

Newtonian mechanics: For the clarification of what is called Newtonian mechanics, or classical mechanics, it is appropriate to distinguish between, on the one hand, the description of the motions of bodies that was first developed by Newton in his work *Philosophiae Naturalis Principia Mathematica* from 1686 and on the other, the *metaphysical superpositions* upon Newton's work.

Newton's *Principia* deals with the *positions* in space of *bodies* and the way these positions change in time, that is the *velocities* of the bodies, and additionally the changes of the velocities, the *accelerations*. The positions are described with the aid of numbers, typically distances between bodies. In the description enters also that which is denoted the *masses* of bodies. The mass is a number which is characteristic of each body and which may be determined by weighing the body.

In Newton's mechanical description the mutual motions of the different bodies are related through something called *forces*, that are said to act upon each body. Forces can be neither seen nor heard. They are nothing more than quantities that may be calculated. The forces enter into a mathematical equation, the *equation of motion*, which tells how the forces that may be calculated have relation to the way each body moves.

The equation of motion says that the magnitude of the force acting upon a body is equal to the mass of the body multiplied by the acceleration of the motion of the body. This equation by itself says nothing about how the bodies move. Not until we have an independent way of calculating the forces, a way that does not merely start from the accelerations and then make use of the equation, will we obtain something new. Newton's trump card here was the force of gravitation. It acts, says Newton, mutually between any pair of bodies, such that the gravitational forces acting upon the two bodies have the same magnitude and are mutually directed towards one another. The magnitude of the force of gravity decreases proportionally to the second power of the distance between the bodies.

Another kind of force is elasticity, for example the force exerted by an expanded string.

When several forces act upon the same body they have to be combined into one resulting force with the aid of a particular rule of calculation. For example, as I sit on my chair this moment Newtonian mechanics will describe me crudely, taken to be a rigid whole, by saying that there is a gravitational force downwards towards the Earth, in addition to an elastic pressure force upwards from the seat of my chair. These two forces are of the same magnitude and in opposite directions. Combining them the resulting force is found to be zero.

When we have calculated the resulting force acting upon a body we may use the equation of motion to determine the acceleration in the motion of the body, that is the momentary change of the velocity. Applied to me sitting in my chair the equation of motion says that my acceleration, like the resulting force acting upon me, is zero, that is to say that my velocity will not change with time. Since my velocity relative to the things in my room also happens to be zero at this moment, Newtonian mechanics tells that I will remain in my chair without motion.

All this implies that if we know the velocity of a body at a certain moment, we will be able by calculation to follow the motion of the body a small step ahead in time and also calculate how the velocity will be when this small step has been taken. The solution of this calculation problem was developed by Newton in the form of the differential and integral calculus (see *mathematical analysis*). With this technique it is then possible to calculate how a number of bodies will continue to move between one another, if only the positions and velocities of all the bodies at one moment are given.

Newton and his successors applied his form of mechanical description to the motions of the planets and the Moon and to various motions in terrestrial scale, such as swinging pendulums. They found that this description agreed well with a series of phenomena of motion, such as they may be observed. In particular the orbital motions of the planets around the Sun, which had been determined by Kepler from Tycho Brahe's observations, displayed striking agreement with Newton's description.

It must be made clear, however, that neither Newton's mechanics nor any other mathematical-physical description of any circumstances of the world has ever agreed with the results of measurements of the state of the world in any logical sense. The agreement which is sought and obtained is always merely *approximate* (for examples see *philosophy of science, physics*).

That Newton's mechanics may only be tested approximately ought not to cause wonder. First of all, the application of the Newtonian descriptive elements to circumstances of the world is by no means a simple matter. In practice the attention must be concentrated upon the main features of certain types of motion, in the first place the motions of the planets around the Sun, the motion of the Moon around the Earth, swinging pendulums, and orbits of projectiles. The phenomena that are amenable to description by Newton's mechanics form only a very small fraction of the properties of the world (see for example the remarks about tides under *determinism*). As an additional circumstance, the application of Newtonian mechanics to the world around us poses mathematical problems that mostly can only be solved approximately.

In spite of its clear limitations, Newton's mechanics was immediately appropriated by the philosophers who in the spirit of Aristotle sought for the highest, ultimate truth about the world. In Newton's mechanics, they said, we have this ultimate truth. Everything in the world may be understood as matter moving in the manner that Newton's equation of motion expresses. Such a philosophical claim is a metaphysical superposition upon Newtonian mechanics.

From this kind of philosophy a metaphysical mystique that claims support from Newtonian mechanics has developed, see for instance *determinism*.

The philosophical idea that everything in the world may be described as matter in motion is curious. The positive inspiration for it is a severely limited field of experience, to wit, the motions of the planets and a few terrestrial phenomena, such as swinging pendulums. Side by side with what is experienced as matter in motion we experience a multitude of everyday phenomena, light, sounds, the various qualities of matter: hardness, colors, weight, and others. And further, as the most important, the experience of being a human being in this world, the thoughts and feelings that fill every one of our wake moments. How all this should be described as matter in motion is left totally in the dark by a philosophy claiming to understand everything in terms of Newtonian mechanics.

After Newton the attempt to describe the world entirely as matter in motion has had to be shelved for many phenomena. This happened first for light and electricity. Through the study of atoms it has become clear that even for matter the matter-in-motion description fails.

See also *spiritism*. Further references are given in the Literature Appendix.

Nonsense: The word is used here about statements that comprise words and phrases that in the stylistic context in which they are used are denotations, but that in the particular context of the statements do not denote anything clearly. In philosophical context nonsense is often found with such denotations as *being, essence, knowledge, language, logic, reality,* qq.v.

Object: The word is used here to denote *thought object* (see *stream of thought*), as by William James.

Objectivity: The word enters into the philosophers' explanation of certain *–isms*. Thereby these become as unclear as the word objectivity.

Occasionalism: Is defined in *Dictionary of Philosophy* as a theory of knowledge and of voluntary control of action, in which mind and matter are non-interactive but events in one realm occur in correspondence with events in the other realm. The explanation is unclear with its talk of mind and matter outside of any context. See also *–ism*.

Octopus in pile of rags: Metaphor for the thought activity, see *stream of thought*.

Paradigm: Paradigm is one of the more recent cries in the scientific sensationalism. When a researcher nowadays is really keen on digging deep into the public research funds one may be fairly certain that he will speak loudly about the paradigm shift his research is about to bring forth.

The paradigm nonsense was launched by Thomas Kuhn in his book *The Structure of Scientific Revolutions*. He maintained here that the development of each science must be understood as a series of periods of what he calls normal science, during which the science in question builds upon a so-called paradigm, each period of normal science replacing another in a crisis, a paradigm shift.

That all this is nonsensical is evident from the fact that nobody, not even Kuhn himself, has been able make clear what in this context the word paradigm denotes. In his later writings Kuhn talks as if theory and paradigm are the same. This is no help since theory is just as unclear as paradigm. It appears that in both cases Kuhn sees them as Aristotelian-logical beings that may be true or false.

The most important thing Kuhn is dealing with in his talk about paradigms consists at closer look of the *description forms* that are made use of in every scientific description. These forms, that is the terms, forms of figures, tables, models, etc., that are used to describe the aspect of the world of concern, are certainly scientifically of the highest importance. Every scientist engaged on formulating a contribution has to choose the description form. When doing so it will often happen that he or she will find it appropriate to join descriptive elements to those that have already been used in the field. In this way the forms that are used in a particular field continue to be developed. A comprehensive revision of the forms being used will of course be felt to be a drastic step, and will often be related to significant new insight. As an example may be mentioned Bohr's description of the hydrogen atom from 1913. In Bohr's description there were no moving particles as in a Newtonian description. Instead Bohr talked about stationary states, see *description form*.

Further references are given in the Literature Appendix.

Peano's axioms: A form of description of the whole numbers. See *mathematical logic*.

Perception: Perception denotes the mental function of conceiving details in the world around us through the senses, for example to see a chair standing at the table, or to hear a blackbird singing. This function is obviously of central importance to any person, practically all the time. Philosophers' description of how perception takes place may upon closer analysis be found to be revealing of their confusion. As illustration the description of perception presented by Bertrand Russell, the leading mathematical logician of his time, will here be taken up.

In his book *The Analysis of Mind*, Lecture V, Russell discusses how a person's perception of ordinary things, such as chairs and tables, has to be understood. He says:

> 'When several people simultaneously see the same table, they all see something different; therefore "the" table, which they are supposed all to see, must be either a hypothesis or a construction. ... It was natural, though to my mind mistaken, to regard the "real" table as the common cause of all the appearances which the table presents (as we say) to different observers. But why should we suppose that there is some one common cause of all these appearances? ... Instead of supposing that there is some unknown cause, the "real" table, behind the different sensations of those who are said to be looking at the table, we may take the whole set of these sensations (together possibly with certain other particulars) as actually *being* the table. ... When different people see what they call the same table, they see things which are not exactly the same, owing to difference of point of view, but which are sufficiently alike to be described in the same words, so long as no great accuracy or minuteness is sought. These closely similar particulars are collected together by their similarity primarily and, more correctly, by the fact that they are related to each other approximately according to the laws of perspective and of reflection and diffraction of light. I suggest, as a first approximation, that these particulars, together with such correlated others as are unperceived, jointly *are* the table; and that a similar definition applies to all physical objects.'

At first sight this account may seem impressive, as deep philosophical insight of the kind one expects from an expert of mathematical logic who takes upon himself to guide us naive laymen. Unfortunately one will find upon closer look that it does not hang together, the whole passage is nonsense. Let us find out how it fails.

Let us start with the explanation of how 'these closely similar particulars are collected together by their similarity primarily and, more correctly, by the fact that they are related to each other approximately according to the laws of perspective and of reflection and diffraction of light.' This explanation, which Russell presents as the very core of the way people perceive things around them, is hardly a model of clarity. Who or what collects something together, and who or what makes use of the laws quoted, and how? As far as I can see it has to be understood such that what Russell calls different appearances of the table, through a mental computation process undergo a detailed analysis, somewhat similar to the computation an engineer has to perform in constructing the perspective in a drawing. This computation then has to make use of the laws quoted.

Concerning this construction one may first be puzzled about the use of the laws of reflection and diffraction of light. Such laws were not known before the time of modern physics. But people readily saw things around them before that time. How could that be?

It must therefore be clear that if Russell's construction is to make sense, the mental computation process Russell talks about must take place without the person's knowing, since none of us is aware of any computation process when we move around among things. Thus according to Russell we must unawares master the laws of reflection and diffraction of light.

When I see a table my insensible computation process according to Russell has the following task: a certain moment my eyes register a certain figure; a bit later my eyes register another figure; now my computation process must compare the two figures and ascertain that they may be understood as two perspectives of one and the same spatial thing, the table.

But how can my insensible computation process know which two figures it has to compare? I continually turn my eyes towards numerous things of many sorts. The table is only one of these things. The answer to the question is that the insensible computation process can only go to work if it already knows which two figures belong to the same thing. But if it knows that the computation process need not go to work, the answer is already given. Thus there is no need for a computation process, and no need for knowledge about the laws of reflection and diffraction. Russell's construction is therefore superfluous, besides being impossible.

This conclusion is confirmed by the fact that people readily recognize a table they see on a picture, where they cannot make use of any three dimensional perspective.

A corresponding confusion is found in Russell's saying that 'When different people see what they call the same table, they see things which are not exactly the same, owing to difference of point of view, but which are sufficiently alike to be described in the same words'. But how is 'described in the same words' to be understood? Even when the word spoken is the same, the sounds brought forth are never quite the same, particularly when spoken by different persons. Thus Russell has to assume that people immediately are able to recognize the same word, even in different pronunciations. But then we may surely recognize the same table, even seen from different sides. Besides we are readily able to recognize things even when we do not have designations for them. Thus Russell's presumptuous beating about the bush is an expression of a defect understanding of perception.

With the above critical analysis as background we shall now look more closely at Russell's first words: 'When several people simultaneously see the same table, they all see something different'. Here Russell manages to talk plain nonsense, simply by his inability to hold on to the meaning of a word within a single sentence. The word is 'see'. Russell is evidently unable to distinguish between perception, which is concerned with the understanding a person achieves through the senses, and the processes of various kinds that enter into sensation. When Russell says 'they all see something different' he clearly has in mind such matters as the image the person's eye lens forms upon the retina of his eye. This image is undoubtedly different in different persons, even when they see the same table. With his manner of speaking Russell must understand seeing to consist in the person seeing an image formed on the person's retina. But if this is to be a valid way to understand seeing, if follows immediately that the person has to be equipped with a kind of mental lens that forms an image of the image on the retina, and thus a further mental lens seeing the image of the image formed ... etc. *in infinitum*. Without himself noticing it, the famous mathematical logician has embarked upon an infinite regression, an infinity of mental lenses and images. Russell's construction is impossible.

Russell's middle passage says: 'Instead of supposing that there is some unknown cause, the "real" table, behind the different sensations of those who are said to be looking at the table, we may take the whole set of these sensations (together possibly with certain other particulars) as actually *being* the table.' Here we have then the Aristotelian metaphysician hunting 'the "real" table' or what the table really *is* (q.v.). And the result is that the table is 'the whole set of these sensations (together possibly with certain other particulars)'. I have to admit that I can assign no meaning to this talk of the real table, or the table as it is, it is to me empty squabble.

It may further be noted that Russell's theory of perception is totally powerless in the face of perception called forth by sounds, for example spoken words or the sound from a whistle.

As a further objection it should be noted that if Russell's discussion is to make sense it has to build on the assumption that 'seeing an appearance' is an isolated, primitive experience. His discussion is blind to the experience of the stream of thought, which presents to us, not isolated things, but an ever changing panorama of something visible, sounds, touch sensations, smells, taste, visual images, imagined sounds and voices, and more. Normally a person does not see a table, or the appearance of a table. The person will experience a furnished room, with many different things, and in addition a fly buzzing around, a curtain floating in the breeze that is felt coming from the open window, in addition to the mental images, all of them with their fringes of feelings. The experience further includes an immediate awareness of the immediate past and of what is about to take place.

What has to be accounted for is not how a few appearances of a table are combined, but the fact that the person in this buzzing confusion will distinguish any number of separate parts of the panorama experienced, such as things, buzzing flies, and breezes. Without such an account Russell's theory of perception is void of coherent sense.

Russell's defective theory of perception is taken directly over in so-called *artificial intelligence.*

The defects of Russell's theory of perception stand in even sharper relief upon comparison with William James's description of mental life in his *Principles of Psychology*. James's description of perception coheres primarily in virtue of the basic characteristic of mind that James calls *the constancy in the mind's meanings*. The mind can always intend, and know when it intends, to think of the Same, something the mind's thought object is *acquainted with*, see *concept, knowing*. The person notices the fly's buzzing, which turns the thought to the same buzzing produced by other flies.

James's description accounts for the perception of definite matters, such as things, by combining the constancy in the mind's meanings with associations. A brief, limited sensation through association turns the person's thought to something already more fully known as a constant meaning, something moreover that the person habitually has encountered in the situation and therefore expects. During the experience of an ordinary scene with things and happenings, the person's state of thought will change incessantly, the *attention* will jump around. Through this changing attention any matter that is known to be the same as something already known may be distinguished.

According to James's description of perception (*Principles of Psychology,* II p. 82) it holds that

> '*where the sensation is associated with more than one reality,* so that either of two discrepant sets of residual properties may arise, the perception is doubtful and vacillating, and *the most that can then be said of it is that it will be of a* ·PROBABLE *thing.*'

This may be confirmed at the experience of faulty perception. For example in the dark something faintly and partly seen may be visually perceived to be one thing; then when something more of it becomes visible the perception may abruptly change to something else instead. Both before and after the change the thing is perceived fully, not just as an unidentified appearance.

What is special about *things* in the stream of thought is their relative permanence, a characteristic experienced as a feeling in their fringe in the stream of thought, see *feeling, stream of thought, thing.*

James's principle, the constancy in the mind's meanings, accounts for the person's recognition of the sameness of not only things such as tables, but of words, of clouds drifting over the sky, of tones of voice, of persons, etc. etc. By comparison Russell's construction is seen to be entirely inadequate by insisting that perception depends on the laws of physics. As a matter of fact, the kinds of changes in the visual appearance, feeling to the touch, and emission of sound, that enter into a person's ordinary perception of the matters in the surroundings of daily life, are far too complicated to make possible even just crude description by present day physics. Physics provides no basis for Russell's pompously philosophical dismissal of the ordinary experience, that people do in fact see such things as tables.

James stresses: what is known is the sameness of 'the mind's meanings', not of things (see *concept*). The buzzing of a fly may at any time be perceived to be the same as the buzzing of other flies at other occasions, without implying any sameness, neither of the fly, nor of the actually buzzing, if it even makes sense to talk of that.

See also *cause, language, language-as-something-fallacy, psychology.* Further references are given in the Literature Appendix.

Phenomenalism: Defined in *Dictionary of Philosophy* as theory that knowledge is limited to phenomena including (a) physical phenomena or the totality of objects of actual and possible perception and (b) mental phenomena, the totality of objects of introspection. The definition is unclear by its talk of knowledge and of objects of perception and of introspection. See also *–ism, knowing, knowledge.*

Philosophy: Philosophy goes back to Aristotle. He described the historical development of civilization in terms of five main stages. The fourth stage is concerned with the study of the material causes of existing things. The fifth stage reaches divine philosophy, when the mind grasps the formal and final causes of things. The fifth stage is of course the highest, and whoever deals with that will be superior to all others in insight. Thus philosophers are *presumption* incarnate. Hence the clinging to Aristotle's ideas that thrives among philosophers until today.

Ryle, *The Concept of Mind*, p. 303, puts it in this way:

'Philosophers have promised to give an account of the World as a Whole, and to arrive at this account by some process of synoptic contemplation. In fact they have practised a highly proprietary brand of haggling.'

More descriptively philosophy may be characterized thus: A form of literature specially characteristic by two traits: (1) Texts of the form employ words and phrases commonly used in daily life, but uses them without indicating a context that might make them meaningful. Thus the form builds upon unclarity, and opens a rich field of empty controversy. (2) The interest is centered upon statements that are assumed to be true or false. There is no place for description, for giving expression to selected properties of matters.

Philosophy of science: The talk of a philosophy of science mainly goes back to John Stuart Mill. His contribution was presented in a book titled *A System of Logic* from 1843. Here he talks about how to prove that scientific theories are true. His main headache in this context is to ascertain how a series of observations of particular instances of a certain phenomenon may be taken to be the basis of a logical proof of the validity of a rule or law that holds generally, for all instances, so-called induction from special cases. This problem has also troubled later philosophers. Karl Popper in his book from 1935, *Logik der Forschung,* turns the problem around, and says that one cannot prove that a law is true, but one may by an experiment show that it is false.

All this talk of truth in science rests on a misconception of what happens in scientific work. The philosophers of science do not notice that scientists in their real work do not concern themselves with philosophical truth. For example when the mathematician Carl Friedrich Gauss in 1801 had a scientific triumph by successfully calculating the position of the newly discovered planet Ceres, it was not the case that his prediction was correct. Predictions never are, there are always deviations from what is found by measurements.

Ceres was discovered by chance on 1801 January 1 and was observed repeatedly during the following months, as it moved slowly among the other stars from night to night. But then it came close to the Sun in the sky, and therefore could not be seen for several months. In order to find the planet in the sky many months later, when it had passed behind the Sun, it was therefore necessary to determine its orbit around the Sun from observations covering a period of a few months. This was the problem solved by Gauss. Guided by his results the planet was then recovered in the sky the following winter.

This was a great scientific triumph, but it rested on no kind of logic. The orbit calculated by Gauss had nothing to do with truth. As Gauss himself knew perfectly well, his calculation of the orbit of Ceres only took the gravitation from the Sun into account, while it ignored the gravitation from the other planets, the Earth, Jupiter, etc. Thus his calculation was known beforehand to be merely an approximation to the best insight at the time into the motions of the solar system. And again this insight was no expression of truth, but merely had proved to allow useful, but by no means logically correct, predictions of the positions of the planets in the sky.

The ground of Gauss's success was that the numbers resulting from his orbit calculation *were good enough* to make the recovery of the planet possible. The astronomer who tried to make the recovery did not expect that Gauss's numbers should fit perfectly. He undoubtedly investigated the stars that were visible in a certain area of the sky, around the place Gauss had determined by calculation, in order, if possible, to find a star that moved from one night to the next, approximately in the way Ceres should be seen according to Gauss's calculation. And this was what he found.

But how to prove logically that the star he found *really* was Ceres? One might as well ask how to prove logically that the pencil now lying before me on my table is the same as the one I had in my hand two minutes ago. These are the kinds of question that philosophers busy themselves about.

That which physicists are dealing with for the philosophers of science has a holy status. By the way things are presented by philosophers one will get the impression that real science is physics, and perhaps chemistry. Besides these the philosophers' star gallery has mathematical logic, but that again is a matter of a different character. But other fields, such as astronomy, geology, meteorology, zoology, and botany, are inconvenient for the philosophers of science. The point is that it cannot be hidden that at least astronomy has had striking successes with such predictions that warm a philosopher's heart. But the astronomers do not make experiments, that which to a philosopher is the core of science. The remaining fields, geology, meteorology, zoology, and botany, cannot boast, neither of the accuracy of their predictions, nor of their experiments. Are these fields not rather poor, scientifically? The best course for the philosopher of science is probably just to forget about them.

And such a field as psychology—Popper shudders at the mere mention of it. This goes back, he tells himself, to the excitement about Freud's psychoanalysis in Vienna in the 1920es, see *psychology*.

To the philosopher physics is a matter of true theories. Popper in the first words of *The Logic of Scientific Discovery* puts it this way 'A scientist, whether theorist or experimenter, puts forward statements, or systems of statements, and tests them step by step.' To this is to be said merely that this description of the activity of scientists is totally misleading, see *law of nature, scientific-scholarly activity*.

See also *mathematical analysis*. Further references are given in the Literature Appendix.

Physics: To philosophers of science physics is the only respectable scientific field (see *philosophy of science*), and the philosophers use the phrase 'the laws of physics' in their explanations of certain –isms in such a way that it is implied that thereby they refer to something that is incontestably true or correct. These locutions confuse the understanding of what physicists have in fact contributed.

If instead of blinding oneself by Aristotelian truth one proceeds empirically and considers what physicists do in fact deal with, one will find that they, like many other scientists and scholars, such as for example chemists, biologists, sociologists, anthropologists, and linguists, are concerned with formulating *descriptions of certain aspects of what we find around us*. What distinguishes the various scientific fields is which kind of aspect is described. The domain of physics are *phenomena that repeat themselves*. Thus it becomes clear that physics goes across most other fields, so to speak, in other words that in certain sides of what scientists from other fields are dealing with there is something of interest to physicists. This has been particularly prominent in the close contact between physics, chemistry, and astronomy, and is reflected in such denotations as astrophysics and physical chemistry.

Physics ...

Thus each of the descriptions established by physicists will be valid for a whole class of phenomena, to wit all phenomena of a certain kind that may be seen as repeat performances of one another. For example the physicists have noted that in the swinging of something heavy suspended in a string there is something that repeats itself, no matter what the heavy thing is made from. So the physicists may in one stroke describe the swinging of all pendulums. But anything in the world has an infinity of properties. Consequently no physical description may be complete. *And no description is exact*, there are always deviations between what a physical description says about the way of the world and what is found by measurements of the aspect under review. This holds for the classical mechanics and gravity, as well as for the theory of relativity, the theory of atoms, and quantum mechanics. Talking, as the philosophers of science incessantly do, as though a description in physics (a so-called 'physical theory' or 'law of nature') may be shown to be either true or false is nonsense.

If, as Popper, one is interested in whether a physical theory may be falsified, one need take no trouble. The answer is given beforehand, to wit that the theory logically is false. Whichever measurement one might think of carrying out will show deviations from what the theory says.

As illustration we may take a matter that has been decisive to the whole of Popper's philosophy of science, to wit the measurements of positions of stars whose light has passed close by the Sun during a total eclipse of the Sun. This light has been influenced by the field of gravity of the Sun, whereby the positions observed from the Earth have shifted relative to the positions of the stars observed when the Sun is not close by. These shifts were an important matter for Einstein's general theory of relativity from 1916, since they are among the very few phenomena where what is found from Einstein's theory deviates measurably from what is found from Newtonian mechanics. The results of the measurements of the positions of the stars have been reproduced below from Einstein's *Über die spezielle und die allgemeine Relativitätstheorie* from 1921.

Shifts in the positions of stars
caused by the gravitation from the Sun
measured during the eclipse of the Sun on 1919 May 29
Unit of measurement: second of arc
(1 degree = 3600 seconds of arc)

Number of star	First coordinate measured	computed	Second coordinate measured	computed
11	-0.19	-0.22	+0.16	+0.02
5	-0.29	-0.31	-0.46	-0.43
4	-0.11	-0.10	+0.83	+0.74
3	-0.20	-0.12	+1.00	+0.87
6	-0.10	-0.04	+0.57	+0.40
10	-0.08	+0.09	+0.35	+0.32
2	+0.95	+0.85	-0.27	-0.09

The issue is to compare the numbers given in the columns 'measured' and 'computed'. If Einstein's theory were to be declared true these numbers ought to be pairwise equal. As may be seen this is not satisfied for a single one of the 14 pairs. The deviations range between 0.01 for star 4 in the first coordinate and 0.18 for star 2 in the second coordinate.

Einstein comments these results by saying: 'The result of the measurement confirmed the theory in a fully satisfactory manner.' This way of expression is typical of defensible *scientific* formulation. Einstein does *not* say that the results of the measurements prove something, or that something is true. What is scientifically interesting is how the theory describes some observable aspect of the world, and whether it describes it better than another theory. In the present case the issue is whether Einstein's description is better than Newton's. By Newton's description the light rays will also be bent close to the Sun, but the shift in positions will only be half of what they are by Einstein's theory. The interesting point is therefore whether the shifts that have been measured agree better with the numbers that have been computed by Einstein's theory or with numbers that are half as great. Doing the calculation one will find that Newton's numbers overall fit considerable worse than do Einstein's. The biggest deviation of Newton's numbers is 0.56, which is considerably bigger than the number 0.18 we found above. It is this better agreement which Einstein calls fully satisfactory.

According to Popper's logistic understanding the measurements from the eclipse of the Sun constitute a 'crucial test', a test such that if it fails it will imply that the theory has to be rejected. This way of describing the situation is a philosophical conceit. The scientist Einstein sees the matter quite differently. As a matter of fact Einstein has searched eagerly for detectable differences between Newtonian mechanics and the theory of relativity, but has only found three (Einstein: *Über die spezielle und die allgemeine Relativitätstheorie*, 1921, pp. 85-91): The change of the direction of the perihelion of the orbit of Mercury, the bending of light rays in a gravitational field, and the red shifts of spectral lines in a gravitational field. Quite apart from that the general theory of relativity describes only a certain aspect of the world—it cannot describe electricity and atoms—so it is obviously not true. Accordingly Einstein continued for many years to search for better theories.

The great attention given to this situation is due, not to scientific concerns, but to *philosophical*. The sensation is that Einstein comes along and says that Newton's theory is not true! In relation to scientific description the matter is slight. Einstein presents a *form of description* which is quite different from Newton's. This form is practically unmanageable, it leads to unsolvable mathematical problems and is only used to make guesses about what happened 15 billion years ago and suchlike. It never gives the same results as Newton's theory, but the deviations between the results of the two theories may be shown to be so slight as to be hidden in the uncertainty of the measurements, with a few exceptions.

See also *–ism, law of nature*. Further references are given in the Literature Appendix.

Plato: See *foundations.*

Poincaré , Henri: See *consciousness.*

Popper, Karl: The Aristotelian-logistic understanding of science in recent times has been put forward particularly by Karl Popper, primarily in his book *Logik der Forschung* (English title: *The Logic of Scientific Discovery*). The background of the book Popper himself has described in *Conjectures and Refutations*. He tells how he arrived at his understanding under the impression of two issues, the one being the investigation of Einstein's theory of relativity during the eclipse of the Sun in 1919, the other being the debate over Freud's psychoanalysis.

According to Popper's view Einstein's theory of relativity was tested logically through observations at the eclipse of the Sun in 1919, and he sees this situation as the prototype of what science is about. This Popperian presentation is entirely misleading, both in relation to what happened in 1919 and in relation to science generally. For more of this, see *physics*.

Popper presents the situation around the theory of relativity in contrast to the debate over Freud's psychoanalysis, which in his view stamps psychology as being unscientific. With this attitude Popper precludes himself from being concerned with the relation of knowing between human beings and their surroundings, and thus he bases his book *The Logic of Scientific Discovery* upon a fallacious understanding of the scientific activity, see *philosophy of science*.

See also *psychology, scientific-scholarly activity*. Further references are given in the Literature Appendix.

Program control: See *Turing*. Further references are given in the Literature Appendix.

Programming language: See *formal language*. Further references are given in the Literature Appendix.

Proof: See *logic, mathematical logic*.

Property: That which comes to us in our stream of thought we experience at first, in our first days of life, as a *buzzing confusion*. Our discrimination of *properties*, such as faces, things, color, sound, hardness, shape, size, heaviness, develops gradually, particularly during our early years of life, through our having the opportunity to compare various buzzing confusions in our thought. The discrimination of a property of an experienced whole is a matter of practice. A large part of any education consists in sharpening the students' discrimination of properties of certain wholes that are of special interest in a certain context. For example the education in music to a large part consists in learning to discriminate properties of something heard. Thus the same piece of orchestral music, when heard simultaneously be several listeners, will be perceived by the listeners to have quite different properties. A musically untrained person perhaps will only perceive the changing overall sound and the melodies. A more trained person may in the total sound be able to pick out the sounds of the individual instruments, here it is the oboe, here the violins, etc. and may be able to identify the harmonies formed by the tones.

Aristotle's philosophy builds upon the notion that some properties are better than others, see *essence*. See also *truth*.

Psychology: Psychology will here be taken to denote the description of human thought activity. Psychology has throughout history and until today been closely tied to what is called philosophy, in such a way that in many historically famous contributions it is impossible to distinguish between philosophy and psychology. Through this close connection psychology has continually been led astray by philosophical thinking.

To Aristotle psychology was related to philosophy through logic, which allegedly expressed 'the correct thinking'. This coupling was retained in the scholasticism of the Middle Ages. A renewal of Aristotelianism in psychology came with Descartes, in the form of his logic-inspired description of man as a soul in a body, and with John Locke and David Hume, who talked of human experience as being composed of 'elementary ideas'.

A more description-oriented psychology was developed by the English psychologists of the nineteenth century. This development reached its highest point in William James's *Principles of Psychology* from 1890, which rejects Aristotle and philosophy completely. For more of this see *association, concept, fringe, habit, perception, reasoning, stream of thought, thought-as-perception-mistake.*

The great setback happened around 1910 with the launching of *behaviorism.* The behaviorists misunderstood science and interpreted the success of physics as a question of logic, of proving the truth of theories. The behaviorists decreed that the description of the thought activity was unscientific, and any mention of introspection was put under taboo. This attitude dominated much of psychology of the twentieth century. Side by side with this, under the impression of Freud's idea, there thrived a lively interest in the psychology of human intercourse, to such an extent that the vulgar notion is that psychology is merely that.

A further setback to the psychology which is concerned with people's knowing adjustment to the world in which they live happened with the introduction of the computer-inspired psychology, the description of man as an information processor, under such denotations as 'artificial intelligence' and 'cognitive science'. This line directly continues Hume's atomistic psychology (see *artificial intelligence*).

In parallel with this, a view has developed that more or less explicitly maintains that human experience is composed of texts of language, see *thinking-as-language-fallacy.*

Among present day philosophers an amateurish superficiality and ignorance towards psychology is prevalent, see for example *association* (quotation from Ryle), *knowing, perception* (quotation from Russell), *Popper, word-as-code-of-meaning-fallacy* (quotation from Wittgenstein). As illustration we may take the following passage from Eddington, *The Nature of the Physical World,* p. 321:

> '*Symbolic Knowledge and Intimate Knowledge.* May I elaborate this objection to introspection? We have two kinds of knowledge which I call symbolic knowledge and intimate knowledge. I do not know whether it would be correct to say that reasoning is only applicable to symbolic knowledge, but the more customary forms of reasoning have been developed for symbolic knowledge only. The intimate knowledge will not submit to codification and analysis; or, rather, when we attempt to analyse it the intimacy is lost and it is replaced by symbolism.'

This passage from Eddington may be taken as a description of human thinking. As such it is appalling. It makes use of descriptive elements, to wit 'knowledge we have', 'symbolic knowledge', 'intimate knowledge', and 'reasoning', that in the face of what is described, an aspect of human thinking, are entirely misleading. The passage is characteristic of the amateurish way philosophers talk of the thought activity. With its unclear terms and ignorance of what has been established in classical work, in particular that of William James, the passage is unworthy of a scientist.

See also *knowing, philosophy of science, reasoning, stream of thought.* Further references are given in the Literature Appendix.

Quine, W. V.: See *knowing, psychology, thinking-as-language-fallacy.*

Rationality: Aristotle said that the *essence* of man is to be a rational animal, in view of the fact that only human beings speak. However, the fact is merely that people speak habitually. This does not imply that human beings in any way, in speaking or otherwise, behave in accordance with any rule or any principle. Much talk is void of meaningful coherence. Rationality can only be determined as a property of a linguistic utterance, but linguistic activity does not imply any coherence in what is said.

Reading proficiency: It is usually assumed that reading proficiency is well defined and may be attained once for all. In tends to be overlooked, first that reading proficiency is as multifarious as linguistic styles. Linguistic styles differ most markedly in the local vocabulary employed. But there are additional differences that relate to the subject field under discourse, besides personal style differences. It is usually overlooked that *reading proficiency*, like any other proficiency, *is retained only through use and practice*. A person who in daily life reads only newspapers and texts on the TV screen will soon find it difficult or impossible to read through a novel. As a matter of fact even persons who as their regular employment read texts in an academic context may feel totally lost when faced with a message from the tax administration authority.

Reality: 'Reality' is one of the words of a small handful which constitutes the core of the traditional philosophical inanity. The word enters into the philosophers' explanations of certain *isms*. The reality nonsense continues in full force until today. We find for example Finn Collin writing in *Hovedområdet* No. 6, 1997, about 'the whole reality', 'description of reality', 'the absolute description of reality ... is ... "a view from nowhere"', 'physics makes a step towards an absolute description of reality'. In the given context these phrases are void of clear meaning.

Not only philosophers but even significant scientists commit themselves to nonsense about reality. As illustration a section from A. S. Eddington's *The Nature of the Physical World* is discussed below.

The philosophical nonsense appears even in the title of Eddington's book: The Nature of the Physical World. 'The Physical World', what is it, what is he talking about? This denotation is merely a mist. And the book is about the nature of this misty matter. 'Nature' without further explanation again is philosophical obscurity.

Chapter XIII of Eddington's book is titled Reality. This chapter is philosophical inanity throughout, and may serve as a typical example. It opens as follows:

> *'The Real and the Concrete.* One of our ancestors, taking arboreal exercise in the forest, failed to reach the bough intended and his hand closed on nothingness. The accident might well occasion philosophical reflections on the distinctions of substance and void—to say nothing of the phenomenon of gravity. However that may be, his descendants down to this day have come to be endowed with an intense respect for substance arising we know not how or why. So far as familiar experience is concerned, substance occupies the centre of the stage, rigged out with the attributes of form, colour, hardness, etc., which appeal to our several senses. Behind it is a subordinate background of space and time permeated by forces and unconcrete agencies to minister to the star performer.
>
> Our conception of substance is only vivid so long as we do not face it. It begins to fade when we analyse it. We may dismiss many of its supposed attributes which are evidently projections of our sense-impressions outwards into the external world. Thus the colour which is so vivid to us is in our minds and

cannot be embodied in a legitimate conception of the substantial object itself. But in any case colour is no part of the essential nature of substance. Its supposed nature is that which we try to call to mind by the word "concrete", which is perhaps an outward projection of our sense of touch. When I try to abstract from the bough everything but its substance or concreteness and concentrate on an effort to apprehend this, all ideas elude me; ... In the scientific world the conception of substance is wholly lacking, and that which most nearly replaces it, viz. electric charge, is not exalted as star-performer above the other entities of physics.'

The philosophical nonsense is bursting from the seams of this passage. What does it mean that 'the colour which is so vivid to us is in our minds'? This is merely the presumptuous philosopher's nonsense. Or take the last sentence, which says that the conception of substance is lacking in the scientific world and is replaced by electric charge. What is that, 'the scientific world'? As well known, physicists talk a lot about electric charge when they describe the properties of matter. This they began to do around the middle of the nineteenth century. But this has not made them stop talking about other properties of the substances. With the development of physics ever further properties of the substances have been investigated and described. But this does not make it wrong or meaningless to talk of such properties that have been investigated earlier. Irrespective of the discoveries of atomic physics it continues to be fully scientifically valid to deal with for example the elasticity, the surfaces, and the behaviour under heating, etc., of solid substances. Such properties of the substances that have been investigated independently of the theory of atoms remain scientifically interesting, irrespective of development of that theory.

Further, these very electric charges that Eddington talks about only make sense as properties of *something*. This something is the kind of matter we are all *acquainted with*. The talk of a special 'scientific world', in which it makes sense to talk about electric charges, but not about such things we are all acquainted with in daily life, is pure nonsense.

The nonsense in Eddington's discussion stems from the philosophical dogma that something has to be appointed to be essential properties (see *essence*). And why so? Answer: because Aristotle says so. Thus Aristotle says that colour is not an essential property. And so Eddington has to say the same.

But Eddington admits that he does not get anywhere with his twaddle. A few pages after the above quotation he says:

'I am afraid of this word Reality, not connoting an ordinary definable characteristic of the things it is applied to but used as though it were some kind of celestial halo. I very much doubt if any one of us has the faintest idea of what is meant by the reality or existence of anything but our own Egos.'

In these words there is hidden a feeble start towards sensible understanding. It would have become Eddington better if instead of all the previous nonsense he had followed this lead. If so he might have realized that sensible talk about reality must build upon what we *experience* in connection with our talking about reality. The description of this belongs to psychology. Instead of embarking upon his amateurish twaddle Eddington might have consulted the scientific literature. Here he soon ought to have found the classical masterpiece, William James's *Principles of Psychology* with Chapter XXI, *PERCEPTION OF REALITY*. Here James says, among other things (vol. II, pp. 283-308):

'BELIEF. Everyone knows the difference between imagining a thing and believing in its existence, between supposing a proposition and acquiescing in its truth. In the case of acquiescence or belief, the object is not only apprehended by the mind, but is held to have reality. Belief is thus the mental state or function of cognizing reality. As used in the following pages, 'Belief' will mean every degree of assurance, including the highest possible certainty and conviction. ...

... In its inner nature, belief, or the sense of reality, is a sort of feeling more allied to the emotions than to anything else. ... What characterizes both consent and belief is the cessation of theoretic agitation, through the advent of an idea which is inwardly stable, and fills the mind solidly to the exclusion of contradictory ideas. ...

The true opposites of belief, psychologically considered, *are doubt and inquiry, not disbelief. ...*

In every proposition, then, so far as it is believed, questioned, or disbelieved, four elements are to be distinguished, the subject, the predicate, and their relation (of whatever sort it be)—these form the *object* of belief—and finally the psychic attitude in which our mind stands toward the proposition taken as a whole—and this is the belief itself.

Admitting, then, that this attitude is a state of consciousness *sui generis*, about which nothing more can be said in the way of internal analysis, let us proceed to the second way of studying the subject of belief: *Under what circumstances do we think things real? ...*

... all propositions, whether attributive or existential, are believed through the very fact of being conceived, unless they clash with other propositions believed at the same time, by affirming that their terms are the same with terms of the other propositions. ... The whole distinction of real and unreal, the whole psychology of belief, disbelief, and doubt, is thus grounded on two mental facts—first that we are liable to think differently of the same; and second, that when we have done so, we can choose which way of thinking to adhere to and which to disregard.

The subjects adhered to become real subjects, the attributes adhered to real attributes, the existence adhered to real existence; whilst the subjects disregarded become imaginary subjects, the attributes disregarded erroneous attributes, and the existence disregarded an existence in no man's land, in the limbo 'where footless fancies dwell'. The real things are, in M. Taine's terminology, the *reductives* of the things judged unreal.

THE MANY WORLDS. Habitually and practically we do not *count* these disregarded things as existents at all. For them *Væ victis* is the law in the popular philosophy; they are not even treated as appearances; they are treated as if they were mere waste, equivalent to nothing at all. To the genuinely philosophic mind, however, they still have existence, though not the same existence, as the real things. *As* objects of fancy, *as* errors, *as* occupants of dreamland, etc., they are in their way as indefeasible parts of life, as undeniable features of the Universe, as the realities are in their way. ...

The most important sub-universes commonly discriminated from each other and recognized by most of us as existing, each with its own special and separate style of existence, are the following:

(1) The world of sense, or of physical 'things' ...

(2) The world of science, or of physical things as the learned conceive them ...

(3) The world of ideal relations, or abstract truths believed or believable by all ...

(4) The world of 'idols of the tribe', illusions or prejudices common to the race ...

(5) The various supernatural worlds ...

(6) The various worlds of individual opinion, as numerous as men are.

(7) The worlds of sheer madness and vagary, also indefinitely numerous.

Every object we think of gets at last referred to one world or another of this or of some similar list. ... Propositions concerning the different worlds are made from 'different points of view'; and in this more or less chaotic state the consciousness of most thinkers remains to the end. Each world *whilst it is attended to* is real after its own fashion; only the reality lapses with the attention.

THE WORLD OF 'PRACTICAL REALITIES'. Each thinker, however, has dominant habits of attention; and these *practically elect from among the various worlds some one to be for him the world of ultimate realities.* From this world's objects he does not appeal. Whatever positively contradicts them must get into another world or die. The horse, e.g., may have wings to its heart's content, so long as it does not pretend to be the real world's horse—*that* horse is absolutely wingless. For most men, as we shall immediately see, the 'things of sense' hold this prerogative position, and are the absolutely real world's nucleus.
...

In the relative sense, then, the sense in which we contrast reality with simple ·*un*reality, and in which one thing is said to have *more* reality than another, and to be more believed, *reality means simply relation to our emotional and active life.* This is the only sense which the word ever has in the mouths of practical men. *In this sense, whatever excites and stimulates our interest is real.*
...

The object of belief, then, reality or real existence, is something quite different from all the other predicates which a subject may possess. Those are properties intellectually or sensibly intuited. When we add any one of them to the subject, we increase the intrinsic content of the latter, we enrich its picture in our mind. But adding reality does not enrich the picture in any such inward way; it leaves it inwardly as it finds it, and only fixes it and stamps it in to *us.* ... *The fons et origo of all reality, whether from the absolute or the practical point of view, is thus subjective, is ourselves.* ...

We reach thus the important conclusion that *our own reality, that sense of our own life which we at every moment possess, is the ultimate of ultimates for our belief.* ... *Whatever things have intimate and continuous connection with my life are things of whose reality I cannot doubt.* ...

THE PARAMOUNT REALITY OF SENSATIONS. But now we are met by questions of detail. What does this stirring, this exciting power, this interest, consist in, which some objects have? which *are* those 'intimate relations' with our life which give reality? And which things stand in these relations immediately, and what others are so closely connected with the former that (in Hume's language) we 'carry our disposition' also on to them?

In a simple and direct way these questions cannot be answered at all. The whole history of human thought is but an unfinished attempt to answer them. For what have men been trying to find out, since men were men, but just those things: 'Where do our true interests lie—which relations shall we call the intimate and real ones—which things shall we call living realities and which not?' A few psychological points can, however, be made clear.

Any relation to our mind at all, in the absence of a stronger relation, suffices to make an object real. ...

Sensible objects are thus either our realities or the tests of our realities. Conceived objects must show sensible effects or else be disbelieved. ...

Sensible vividness or pungency is then the vital factor in reality when once the conflict between objects, and the connecting of them together in the mind, has begun. ...

THE INFLUENCE OF EMOTION AND ACTIVE IMPULSE ON BELIEF.
... Every exciting thought in the natural man carries credence with it. To conceive with passion is eo ipso to affirm. ...'

See also *belief, mathematical logic*. Further references are given in the Literature Appendix.

Reasoning: The word 'reasoning' is used about certain kinds of thought activity. However, philosophers' talk about reasoning is mostly an unclear mixture of several different things. One is the continued flow of thoughts and feelings (see *stream of thought*), in which the *thought objects* replace one another as an unbroken stream (see Bertrand Russell's account quoted under *belief*). However, it is misleading to use the word reasoning about this process, which happens as an even flow, without definite elements.

Often philosophers use the word reasoning about the connection that pertains between different parts of a logical proof, see *logic*. They speak as though the conclusion of the proof emerged from the premises through a thought process, reasoning, as though the human thought activity consisted of a continued chain of proof constructions. This, however, is misleading talk. 'Logical proof' should be reserved to denote a certain structure in a certain type of expressions, and not be used about something happening.

In Chapter XXII of William James's *Principles of Psychology* reasoning denotes a goal oriented thought activity, such that the person from the situation at hand selects and attends to a property of it that by its character, through further *association*, makes it possible that the desired goal may be reached. Let for example the goal be to find out whether or not the Moon is above the horizon at this moment. Then a skilled reasoner from the state of the world in its multiplicity will be able to select that quite special property which is called the times of the rising and the setting of the Moon at this location on this day. These times may be found in an almanac. What the reasoner finds in the almanac thus shares a similarity with the rising and the setting of the Moon. In virtue of this similarity the data in the almanac enable the reasoner to find the desired answer about the Moon.

James's account of reasoning shows why descriptions, and thereby scholarship and science, are useful to humanity. Through a description of an aspect of the world a reasoner gets access to properties of the aspect that otherwise would remain unnoticed.

See also *association by similarity, description, psychology, scientific-scholarly activity*. Further references are given in the Literature Appendix.

Rubin, Edgar: See *foundations, science*.

Rule of language: See *language-rule-fallacy*.

Russell, Bertrand: See *belief, cause, knowing, logic, mathematical logic, perception, reasoning, thing, thinking-as-language-fallacy, truth, word-as-code-of-meaning-fallacy*. Further references are given in the Literature Appendix.

Ryle, Gilbert: See *association, belief, concept-is-word-fallacy, knowing, know-how, language philosophy, logic, psychology, thought-as-perception-mistake*. Further references are given in the Literature Appendix.

Science: The talk of definite sciences, and the query whether this or that is 'a science', has since the Second World War become a question of money and power. Thick books are published so as to make clear that for example 'cognitive science' is a science and therefore should be supported with research money. In the previous decades the talk of sciences had centered around the philosophers' logic and 'foundations', see *foundations, is, scientific-scholarly activity*.

Further references are given in the Literature Appendix.

Scientific method: The talk of scientific method presupposes that in order that a person may make great scientific discoveries it should be sufficient that the person became aware of some principles of scientific method.

This notion implies a fundamental misunderstanding of human understanding. If the notion were valid it would be possible to become a virtuoso pianist by studying a piano playing tutor, since the principles underlying piano playing are few and simple.

Scientific-scholarly activity: Science is a recurrent theme in philosophical contexts. The theme is frequently made explicit in claims about what constitutes science or how scientists proceed. The Aristotelian philosopher will of course ask about or make claims about what science *is*.

The philosophical talk about science has much unclarity. Since nobody has the copyright of the words we use, anybody may freely talk nonsense about something they call science. To me in the present context the issue is to *choose* a contents for terms containing 'science' that satisfy certain requirements that I think should be adopted. In other words, I am not going to compete with the philosophers about who knows most about what science *is* (q.v.). But I wish to make use of the opportunity to recommend that the denotation 'science', together with others that are similar to it, are used in a certain manner.

The manner I wish to recommend I have chosen with a view to making that which is distinguished by denotations including the root 'science' include most of what *ordinarily has been honoured* by such recognitions as the Nobel Prize; further to making it something that is not restricted to certain particular areas of insight, but *is important to many areas;* and finally to making it something that by its character is of manifest *value to the development of human culture*.

Starting from these concerns I have found, first, that the English term 'science' is inconveniently restrictive in relation to activities that are important to a wide range of areas of insight that are of value to human culture. A more adequate term is 'science and scholarship'. Second I have found that the core of science and scholarship is *descriptions of aspects of the world of a special character,* more particularly descriptions that cohere with other descriptions of aspects of the world, as far as possible across a wide field of aspects. This characteristic of science and scholarship is most conveniently displayed by particular examples. Here the descriptions that were relevant to Francis Crick og James Watson's discovery in 1953 of the molecular structure of DNA shall be displayed. These descriptions are discussed more fully in Watson's book *The Double Helix*.

There are two main ingredients in Crick and Watson's discovery, one is something called DNA, the other is the model of DNA they developed. First about DNA. By this was denoted, in the historical situation and context in which Watson and Crick found themselves in 1950, a substance whose identity and properties may be understood only in their coherence with a vast multitude of chemical and biological descriptions, as these had been developed in the previous centuries by a large number of chemists and biologists. We should avoid the misleading simplification of just saying that DNA is a chemical substance or compound. Any talk of chemical compounds rests upon the use in chemistry of a special *description form*, to wit showing each pure compound (in itself a complicated empirical matter) as a spatial pattern of identical molecules, each made up of atoms held together in pairs by special bonds. This description form has been found empirically to be immensely fruitful for the description of such processes in which substances react with one another and are converted to others.

In this context a specific substance, such as DNA, is determined through *descriptions of properties*, including relevant processes, of aspects of the world. Thus is belongs to the properties of DNA that it occurs in living cells and that it may be isolated from other ingredients of such cells by application of a certain refined microbiological technique.

Through numerous investigations already before 1950 a series of further properties of DNA, here to be denoted P1, P2, ..., had been described. It was clear that the molecules must be enormously long, P1, and that they had to be described as chemically bonded chains of smaller constituents, so-called nucleotides, P2, of which four different, called adenine, thymine, guanine, and cytosine, had been found, P3. The scientific literature already presented graphical pictures, or models, of the molecules of DNA corresponding to such a structure.

Further properties of DNA had been described by Chargaff. On the basis of chemical analyses he had found that the relative amounts of the four kinds of nucleotides formed by disrupting the DNA from cells of a particular organism species always are the same, P4. But these relative amounts are highly different in DNA originating from different species. However, Chargaff's measurements suggested that a general rule holds about these amounts. Denoting the relative number of molecules of adenine, thymine, guanine, and cytosine, by respectively A, T, G, and C, it holds, within the uncertainty of the measurements, that $A = T$ and $C = G$, independently of the species from which the DNA has been taken, P5.

These results illustrate the coherence of descriptions that is here taken to be the core of science and scholarship. Each of the original analysis results, that is the figures of A, T, G, and C, found by measurements of the amounts of nucleotides in DNA taken from a certain biological species, is a description of a property of DNA. The property P4 says that these figures are the same for all individuals of a certain species. Assuming that Chargaff speaks the truth of his results the description P4 thus *coheres with* a series of results of measurements, each of which is a description of a property of DNA. The description P5 again coheres with results of measurements, but this coherence embraces results for different species, not merely for different individuals.

Further properties of DNA had been described mostly by Wilkins and Franklin, thus: DNA may form crystals, P6, and these deflect X rays into a definite reflection pattern. Crick and others were able to show that certain features of this pattern would cohere with a spatial molecular structure having one or more helices, P7, while others showed the presence in the molecule of parallel layers of groups of atoms at a distance of 3.4 Å, P8. This analysis was made in terms of descriptions of the molecular structures and the X rays of forms taken from *mathematical analysis.* So much for the descriptions of DNA available before Watson and Crick presented their model.

Watson and Crick's model was in its original form a kind of sculpture, composed of metal rods and plates. It may be seen on photos from 1953, with the two happy discoverers. It should be understood as a scale model of the spatial positions of the atoms of the DNA molecule in a magnification of about 10^9 times. The new insight contributed by the model is that, understood in a certain way, it coheres with all the properties enumerated above as P1 to P8, and additionally with numerous additional general properties concerning chemical bonds for the atoms that enter into it. The model is the first description of DNA *in such sculptural form* which coheres with so many of the known properties of the substance.

Thus what Watson and Crick have contributed, what was honoured by the Nobel Prize in 1962, is a model description of (an aspect of) DNA. This description coheres to a very high degree with other descriptions of what it describes.

It might appear that the characterization of science and scholarship to be primarily a matter of description would make science and scholarship into something tame and unimportant. Such a view overlooks the power that resides in descriptions of how the world is constituted. This power may in certain contexts be of importance to global policy. The insight possessed by a small handful of physicists in the USA, who around 1944 developed the atom bomb, was more than anything tied to written descriptions. These physicists were located at the same place, Los Alamos in New Mexico, and had daily personal contact. But in spite of this direct access to personal, spoken verbal contact, the written descriptions were the anchors of their insight. A large part of their daily activity consisted in working out written formulations, and it was only by means of written reports that they were able to retain, communicate, and test, their constructive ideas. In this way it was possible that the major part of their insight through espionage might be transferred to physicists in the Soviet Union. As a matter of fact the entire Soviet development of atomic reactors and atom bombs over a period of years was an exact copy of corresponding American constructions. This insight was transferred through about 10.000 pages of documentation, transmitted by spies.

See also *foundations, philosophy of science, Popper, reasoning, science.* Further references are given in the Literature Appendix.

Soul: The word enters into the philosophers' explanations of certain *–isms*. What the word denotes, if anything, people have never been able to agree.

Spiritism: The borderline between science/scholarship and spiritism is not a question of the philosophers' *truth* (q.v.), but of *descriptions*. As long as a certain domain of experience has only be described as a disconnected collection of experiences it is assigned to spiritism. If a description of the experiences is established that shows that groups of them may be described coherently, the domain becomes scientific/scholarly. Thus the border between science/scholarship and spiritism is blurred.

The descriptions of phenomena of the world developed by physicists imply no dismissal of spiritism. Such dismissal rests upon metaphysical superpositions upon these descriptions, for example claims that the descriptions of physics are true or complete of the phenomena.

This further implies that in our attempts to find coherence in that which we may observe about the world we have ample leeway for influences and powers that are unknown in Newtonian mechanics. If one likes to understand some of what happens as a result of an interplay of spirits, soul powers, ghosts, or what else one will call them, one need not feel hampered by Newtonian mechanics or any other of the descriptions of physics.

Splashes over the waves: Metaphor for the thought activity, see *stream of thought*.

Stream of consciousness: See *stream of thought*.

Stream of thought: One of the most conspicuous features of philosophical discussions is the way philosophers are ready to talk about such issues as *thought, feeling, association, knowledge,* without placing them in clear relation to what must be the core of the matter, to wit, *every person's experience of his or her thoughts and feelings.* This lack is particularly striking after William James in his classical *Principles of Psychology* from 1890 under the designations *stream of thought* or *stream of consciousness* has presented a clear and elaborate description of the core of the experience of being a human being.

The philosophers' failing interest in descriptions of the stream of thought is found similarly in the decay of psychology under behaviorism in the twentieth century. This phenomenon is illustrated strikingly by the manner in which the stream of thought is treated in modern handbooks. Thus in *Encyclopædia Britannica* the key phrase 'stream of consciousness' gives reference to merely a very brief mention of how the phrase was introduced by William James, and then to several literary passages from the twentieth century, among which, most prominently, the final monologue in the novel *Ulysses* by James Joyce from 1922. Thus 'the stream of consciousness' is described merely as a sensational new literary technique. But this description is profoundly misleading. 'The stream of consciousness' does not primarily denote a literary conceit, it denotes a fundamental human experience. This experience has been known and has been given artistic expression at all times, for example in the soliloquies of Shakespeare's plays, in the solo arias of operas, in the descriptions in novels of the individuals' meditations. The novelty of the monologue in *Ulysses* is not that it describes the person's stream of thought, but partly that Joyce has chosen to present it as merely a sequence of words without punctuation running over 40 pages, partly that the description includes unveiled accounts of the person's erotic fantasies.

In William James's *Principles of Psychology* the stream of thought denotes something happening in all of our wake moments, to wit our experience of thinking and feeling. The stream of thought is known to every one of us through introspection, that is through our turning the attention inward, towards the way we experience our thoughts and feelings. What we may register through introspection is merely a picture of rough outlines. The stream of thought changes incessantly and has a vast number of details, most of which are present only vaguely, far more than may be seized by introspection.

The stream of thought happens independently of our desire. We may, when we so wish, more or less successfully think of something definite, but we cannot make the stream of thought cease, as experienced by every person suffering from insomnia.

The stream of thought may be described as something that flows, an incessantly changing, complicated mixture of something that may be denoted explicitly as images, sounds and bodily impressions, with additional vague moods and feelings. As stressed by James we do not in the stream of thought experience sharply delimited parts or elements of any kind. At each moment our thought is occupied by something that is complicated, but that is experienced as a whole. These wholes James calls *thought objects*. Within each thought object one may distinguish between something more at the center, that which is the subject of our *attention*, and something that forms a *fringe*.

James in his first overview description indicates 5 properties of the stream of thought: 1) Every thought tends to be part of a personal consciousness. 2) Within each personal consciousness thought is always changing. 3) Within each personal consciousness thought is sensibly continuous. 4) It always appears to deal with objects independent of itself. 5) It is interested in some parts of these objects to the exclusion of others, and welcomes or rejects—*chooses* from among them, in a word—all the while. To this one might add that every thought object embraces *feelings*, including those of the personal well-being, moods and bodily presence.

In its continued changing the stream of thought alternates between substantive states of relative repose and transitive states of rapid change. During the transitive states the changes of the thought objects happen so rapidly that they cannot be seized by introspection.

In the experience of the stream of thought the present moment has a duration of a few seconds. As one thought object fades away by being replaced by another one, it is retained in the fringe of the coming one. Every sudden impression is always experienced as a whole with what was there immediately before it happened.

The denotation *stream of thought* is the result of James's choice. He says (vol. 1 p. 239):

'Consciousness, then, does not appear to itself chopped up in bits. Such words as 'chain' or 'train' do not describe it fitly as it presents itself in the first instance. It is nothing jointed; it flows. A 'river' or a 'stream' are the metaphors by which it is most naturally described. *In talking of it hereafter, let us call it the stream of thought, of consciousness, or of subjective life.*'

With these words James emphasizes the importance to our understanding of choosing our metaphors. Taking the point of departure from this suggestion, three different metaphors for aspects of the mental activity, as described by James, shall be proposed.

Metaphor 1: *The mental activity is like a jumping octopus in a pile of rags.* This metaphor is meant to indicate the way in which the state of consciousness at any moment has a field of central awareness, that part of the rag pile in which the body of the octopus is located. The arms of the octopus stretch out into others parts of the rag pile, those parts presenting themselves vaguely, as the fringe of the central field. The rags of the pile are the mental objects that may come to the conscious awareness. They are of all colors and shapes. The jumping about of the octopus indicates how the state of consciousness changes from one moment to the next.

Metaphor 2: *A person's insight is like a site of buildings in incomplete state of construction.* This metaphor is meant to indicate the mixture of order and inconsistency characterizing any person's insights. These insights group themselves in many ways, the groups being mutually dependent by many degrees, some closely, some slightly. As an incomplete building may be employed as shelter, so the insights had by a person in any particular field may be useful even if restricted in scope. And as the unfinished buildings of a site may conform to no plan, so a person may go though life having incoherent insights.

Metaphor 3: *A person's utterances relate to the person's insights as the splashes over the waves to the rolling sea below.* This metaphor is meant to indicate the ephemeral character of our verbal utterances, their being formed, not as a copy of insight already in verbal form, but as a result of an activity of formulation taking place at the moment of the utterance.

See also *acquaintance, description, habit, introspection, language, logic, psychology, reasoning, thinking-as-language-fallacy, thought-as-perception-mistake, Turing.* Further references are given in the Literature Appendix.

Subconsciousness: See *consciousness.* Further references are given in the Literature Appendix.

Substance: Similar as *matter*, q.v.

Substantive state: See *stream of thought.*

Theory: A theory, in the way philosophers talk, is a unit that may be correct or incorrect, true or false. Typically Popper talks about falsifying a theory, showing that it is false. These locutions have no support in the way the word theory is used in scientific/scholarly contexts. Here a theory is a *description* that covers a certain multiplicity of phenomena in one stroke. Bohr's theory of the hydrogen atom from 1913, for example, was a description that succeeded in tying the frequencies of the light emitted from hydrogen atoms together with the energies of the stationary states in which hydrogen atoms may find themselves. It goes without saying that with this understanding of what a theory is, theories will predominantly be developed in physics and chemistry, the scientific fields that are concerned with phenomena that repeat themselves. However, many famous classical works with 'theory' in their title belong to fields far outside science, thus e.g. *Theory of International Economic Policy, Theory of Social Revolutions,* and *A Theory of Ethics.*

Further references are given in the Literature Appendix.

Thing: Philosophers like to talk about something they call things, and have the word enter into their explanations of certain *–isms*. What they mean thereby they usually make no attempt to clarify, and *Dictionary of Philosophy* says nothing about it. Bertrand Russell talks about things in *The Analysis of Mind*, chapter VII, but gets into the impossible explanation quoted under *perception*.

For a sensible account of things we only have to consult William James's *Principles of Psychology* (vol. 1, p. 224):

> 'But what are things? Nothing, as we shall abundantly see, but special groups of sensible qualities, which happen practically or æsthetically to interest us, to which we therefore give substantive names, and which we exalt to this exclusive status of independence and dignity.'

Thinking: See *stream of thought*.

Thinking-as-language-fallacy: Thus is denoted here the notion that our mental activity mainly consists of a processing of verbal expressions. The fallacy goes with the talk of 'knowledge' in the form of verbal statements. The fallacy is expressed in detail by Bertrand Russell, see *belief*. It is found in Quine's *Word and Object*, p. 3, where he says: 'Actual memories mostly are traces not of past sensations but of past conceptualization or verbalization', and in Eddington's talk of '*Symbolic Knowledge and Intimate Knowledge*', see *psychology*. The fallacy finds expression in Turing's Test, see *Turing*.

The thinking-as-language-fallacy is flatly contradicted by the experience of every author, that the generation of the text in progress is a troublesome process, not merely a copying of something already there. Every word, every sentence, requires a tiring exertion (see the description under *introspection*). This typical author's experience may be understood as a consequence of the fact that the generation of each verbal expression involves a choice that has to be made at the moment of generation. This choice again depends on a merely vague feeling about which property of the matter of concern is to be expressed. Each aspect of the world has an infinity of properties (see *essence*). Giving expression of some of them requires a selection, both of which properties and of which verbal expression.

Thus any verbal formulation involves a situation dependent choice between an indefinite mass of possibilities. Correspondingly any verbal formulation will be incomplete compared with the properties of the matter of concern.

The thinking-as-language-fallacy is closely related to fallacies and lack of understanding about conception and denotation, see *concept*.

For a more tenable understanding than thinking-as-language, see *stream of thought*.

See also *word-as-code-of-meaning-fallacy*. Further references are given in the Literature Appendix.

Thought: See *stream of thought.*

Thought object: See *acquaintance, association, association by similarity, introspection, James, language, language-as-something-fallacy, psychology, reasoning, stream of thought, thinking-as-language-fallacy.*

Thought-as-perception-mistake: Thus may be denoted a form of description of people's experience of their stream of thought which starts from the perception of things around and describes the experience of images as an analogous, inner perception. With this form of description all sorts of empty philosophical questions arise, whether the experience of images can be reliable, whether it gives access to truth.

The mistake was revealed explicitly by William James, who writes (*Principles of Psychology*, vol. 1 p. 224)

'Chapter IX - The Stream of Thought

We now begin our study of the mind from within. Most books start with sensations, as the simplest mental facts, and proceed synthetically, constructing each higher state from those below it. But this is abandoning the empirical method of investigation. No one ever had a simple sensation by itself. Consciousness, from our natal day, is of a teeming multiplicity of objects and relations, and what we call simple sensations are results of discriminative attention, pushed often to a very high degree. It is astonishing what havoc is wrought in psychology by admitting at the outset apparently innocent suppositions, that nevertheless contain a flaw. The bad consequences develop themselves later on, and are irremediable, being woven through the whole texture of the work. The notion that sensations, being the simplest things, are the first things to take up in psychology is one of these suppositions. The only thing which psychology has a right to postulate at the outset is the fact of thinking itself, and that must first be taken up and analyzed.'

See also *psychology, stream of thought*.

Gilbert Ryle's book *The Concept of Mind* is said by himself to be an attack on the notion of man as *the ghost in the machine*. At closer look this is an onslaught on the thought-as-perception-mistake, 60 years after William James. On Ryle's book, see also *consciousness, logic*. Further references are given in the Literature Appendix.

Transitive state: See *stream of thought*.

Truth: Ever since the days of Aristotle the philosophers have found themselves in an unceasing fight with the windmills of truth. Their writings constantly talk about truth, and the word enters into their explanations of many of their –isms. In some of their writings they quarrel about what to understand by truth, without arriving at any consensus.

Truth is of course well known from everyday life, where lying is so popular. In ordinary contexts one talks about truth in connection with something a person says about a specific situation, which by the persons involved is perceived with feelings of uncertainty or conflict. Typically a happening has occurred which is seen as unfortunate or unhappy. The persons who know about the happening may then be asked for accounts about it. Such an account is then truthful or mendacious, depending on how it describes the happening. The border between truth and lie, or falsity, is not taken to be sharp. An account may be unclear, it may be evasive, it may be a white lie. Or it may be a flat lie.

Similar talk about truth may be found in ordinary prose descriptions of the life of individuals, most elaborately in novels. In such descriptions truth is always connected with special uncertainty or doubt whether an account of some specific circumstance of human life is adequate (for the source of this claim, consult the Literature Appendix). For most of the accounts we encounter, such doubt, and thus the question of truth, does not arise.

Thus truth is understood ordinarily as a property of an account of a circumstance of the world of a certain character, often with regard to what action one is going to take about the circumstance.

But in the mouth of philosophers truth is a glorious 'something' they aspire to find, but that they have so far searched for in vain. It is rather pathetic to behold. Bertrand Russell, the crusader of philosophical truth before anybody else, in 1931 was challenged by Will Durant for his reply to the following declaration: 'We are driven to conclude that the greatest mistake in human history was the discovery of truth. It has not made us free, except from delusions that comforted us, and restraints that preserved us; it has not made us happy, for truth is not beautiful ...'. To this Russell answered: 'I do not see that we can judge what would be the result of the discovery of truth, since none has hitherto been discovered.'

From time to time the philosophers succeed in dragging even significant scientists into their truth swamp. A prominent example is Eddington. He made great contributions to astrophysics and relativity theory, but also embarked on books having such titles as *The Philosophy of Physical Science* and *The Nature of the Physical World*. In the latter, from 1928, he discusses what he finds is 'the philosophical outcome of the great changes of scientific thought which has recently come about'. In this book he is greatly concerned with truth.

As a characteristic example of Eddington's agonized hunt for truth we may take a look at his argumentation in Chapter XV, *Science and Mysticism*, of *The Nature of the Physical World*. He starts here by giving a brief description of a section of Lamb's *Hydrodynamics* which deals with generation of waves by wind. Eddington shows some of the mathematical formulas that serve to describe the motion of a liquid and summarizes Lamb's main results.

Eddington continues to tell how at another occasion he also thought of waves on water, but at that time took out another book, with a poem describing an impression of a frozen lake under the light of the night sky. He speaks of the deep impression the poem makes upon him, and says that 'life would be stunted and narrow if we could feel no significance in the world around us beyond that which can be weighed and measured with the tools of the physicist.' But then he continues:

'Of course it was an illusion. We can easily expose the rather clumsy trick that was played on us. Aethereal vibrations of various wave-lengths, reflected at different angles from the disturbed interface between air and water, reached our eyes, and by photoelectric action caused appropriate stimuli to travel along the optic nerves to a brain-centre. Here the mind set to work to wave an impression out of the stimuli. The incoming material was somewhat meagre; but the mind is a great storehouse of associations that could be used to clothe the skeleton. Having woven an impression the mind surveyed all that it had made and decided that it was very good. ... Quite illogically we were glad; though what there can possibly be to be glad about in a set of aethereal vibrations no sensible person can explain. ... It was an illusion. Then why toy with it longer? These airy fancies which the mind, when we do not keep it severely in order, projects into the external world should be of no concern to the earnest seeker after truth. Get back to the solid substance of things, to the material of the water moving under the pressure of the wind and the force of gravitation in obedience to the laws of hydrodynamics. But the solid substance of things is another illusion. It too is a fancy projected by the mind into the external world.'

There was one for you, all you naive laymen, who believe you know something about the things around you, come to the deep philosopher, he will reveal your illusions.

But it is nonsense, Eddington's presumptuous talk of illusions. It is no better than if a philosopher would say to me: You believe you are sitting there in a soft chair; but you are the victim of an illusion, you are in reality sitting in a wooden frame covered with cotton textiles and lacquer. And if philosopher number 2 came along and said: Wrong, in reality you are sitting in a model 92-133 covered with material 2217.

Eddington's talk of illusions stems from the Aristotelian dogma that the things merely 'are' something Aristotle calls their essential properties (see *essence*) and that all other properties are illusions. Eddington himself gets lost in his hunt for the essence. He talks first about the solid substance of things, the material of the water moving. But then he says that the solid substance of things is another illusion. 'We have chased the solid substance from the continuous liquid to the atom, from the atom to the electron, and there we have lost it.'

The dogma of essential properties serves no purpose other than the generation of idle nonsense. As we all know, things have lots of properties, of widely different kinds. Fixing our attention at some of them at a certain moment does not make us the victim of any illusion. Eddington's undulating water has such properties that are described by Lamb's equations, but it may just as fully have the properties the poet has expressed in words. There is here no contradiction or possibility of illusion.

Illusion is a matter of the description of a certain kind of property, for example color. I may see a thing and get the impression that it has a certain color, but then come to realize that it is an illusion, that the color in reality is another one. But the illusion depends on my already being acquainted with the quality, here color, that I am mistaken about.

In the way Eddington pursues the Aristotelian dogma of essential properties in his hunt for truth he gets straight into meaninglessness. He does not notice that even just his comparison of the two descriptions, that of hydrodynamics and that of the poet, *depends upon he himself being acquainted* with what may be denoted 'waves on water' (see *knowing*). A description that talks about electrons neither replaces nor contradicts the talk of waves on water, being in fact entirely dependent upon it. The electrons Eddington talks about are indeed properties of this water (see *property*), being the way they are distinguished before the countless other electrons one might talk about. Eddington's saying that the talk of electrons should make the talk of waves on water the expression of an illusion is nonsense.

In his hunt after the philosophical truth, which just is there without connection to particular circumstances or happenings, Eddington is heading directly into nonsense.

Truth outside of a definite context denotes nothing. See also *mathematical logic, philosophy of science, spiritism*. Further references are given in the Literature Appendix.

Turing, Alan: Alan Turing's two best known writings illustrate in a striking manner the harmful influence of philosophical nonsense upon science/scholarship. The first of them, *On Computable Numbers With an Application to the Entscheidungsproblem*, from 1936, was a scientific pioneer contribution. The second one, *Computing Machinery and Intelligence*, from 1950, was sheer philosophical inanity.

In *On Computable Numbers* Turing as the first studies the properties of the numbers that may be determined by computation. By computation Turing understands a work process such that certain numbers become transformed step by step, the action of each step being given by a set of rules that are fixed for each computation.

By an ingenious procedure Turing succeeds in proving a series of general properties of the numbers that may be computed. Turing's procedure is as follows. He first introduces a very simple way to describe computation processes, that which has subsequently been denoted *Turing machines.* A Turing machine consists of a control unit having access to writing and deleting symbols on an infinitely long tape, and its work consists in passing from one state to the next, among a given finite set of states. The work of the control unit is given by a set of rules. Turing machines differ among each other by the set of rules that control them.

But now Turing takes his brilliant decisive step. He says: it it possible to construct a special Turing machine, what he calls a *universal machine*, with the property that if the universal machine is put to work on a tape on which beforehand the rules that control another Turing machine have been written in a certain way, then the universal machine will perform exactly the same computation as the other Turing machine. So as to substantiate this step he then develops the complete set of rules that will control the universal machine. In this way Turing as the first has demonstrated the basic principle, program control, that has been used in all computers since 1949.

In this work Turing speaks very sparingly about the human thought activity, merely saying at one point that the human memory capacity necessarily is bounded and alluding at another point briefly to the state of mind of a person engaged on computation.

In *Computing Machinery and Intelligence* Turing says that he will consider the question: Can machines think? In considering an answer to it he dismisses discussing what is usually considered to be meant by the two words, 'machine' and 'think'. Instead he replaces the question by another one, which, as he says, 'is closely related to it and is expressed in relatively unambiguous words'. The formulation of this other question builds on what Turing calls 'the imitation game'. It is played by three persons, a man (A), a woman (B), and an interrogator (C) who may be of either sex. The interrogator stays in a room apart from the other two. The object of the game for the interrogator is to determine which of the other two is the man and which is the woman. The interrogator's contact with A and B is merely through typed messages. The man A has the task to mislead C, while B has the object to help C to determine the sexes of the two persons. Now Turing says:

'We now ask the question: "What will happen when a machine takes the part of A in this game?" Will the interrogator decide wrongly as often when the game is played like this as he does when the game is played between a man and a woman? These questions replace the original, "Can machines think?"'

This formulation is later known as *Turing's Test.*

Turing's article is both in its main line and in many details entirely nonsensical. Here merely some of the weakness will be pointed out.

The main question, 'Can machines think?', displays in the way it is formulated a fallacious understanding of human thought activity. The formulation implies through the word 'can' that thinking is something that human beings perform, something that is an expression of a special ability. But Turing's question is nonsense; thinking goes on, it is something experienced by people, not something done by them, see *stream of thought.*

Turing's replacement of the question of thinking by a test is an expression of Aristotelian logic fixation. The property 'thinking' is understood in Turing's Test to be something that may be characterized logically, something characterized by a statement being true or false.

Turing's restriction of the contact between the interrogator and A and B to take place merely by typed messages is an expression of the *thinking-as-language-fallacy*, q.v. This restriction is obviously chosen by Turing so as to prevent the interrogator C from an ordinary immediate determination of the sexes of the two persons from their looks, tones of voice and appearance. Only under this arbitrary restriction the reactions of a machine might have any chance of holding its own in the game.

Turing's description of the terms of the test is unclear. He starts by saying that the interrogator C has the object to determine the sexes of A and B. But if A is replaced by a machine it makes no sense to talk of A's sex. It is unclear whether it should be made clear to C that the real object is to distinguish a machine from a human being.

By saying that his test demonstrates a property of a machine Turing confuses the understanding of who would deserve the credit if the test succeeded. The credit should be given, not to the machine but to the person who wrote the program for it.

Turing's argumentation in *Computing Machinery and Intelligence* has had great influence on the later talk of *artificial intelligence*, q.v. In this way the article has contributed to infecting computing with nonsense.

Further references are given in the Literature Appendix.

Turing machine: See *Turing*. Further references are given in the Literature Appendix.

Turing's Test: See *Turing*.

Unconscious: See *consciousness*.

Understand-fallacy: This is the mistaken notion that people have the same understanding of the words they habitually share. The understand-fallacy is closely related to the *word-as-code-of-meaning-fallacy* and the *thinking-as-language-fallacy*.

The understand-fallacy finds various expression. One is the misunderstanding that people generally understand what they are told and what they read. Another expression of the fallacy is the talk of illiteracy as a sharply defined property of each person.

'Understanding' has useful meaning only a designation of something individual, personal, something that is situation, including life situation, dependent. It is meaningless to say that two persons have the same understanding of something.

A person's understanding of a verbal expression cannot be distinguished sharply from the same person's understanding of all other kinds of expression. The intercourse of people consists of the interchange of expressions of many kinds, of which words merely make out a part.

People undoubtedly understand only a fraction of what they hear and read. Verbal expression comes in countless different styles, of which each is tied to a definite kind of situation. Each style requires for its understanding a habitual proficiency which for its maintenance has to be practised regularly, like any other know-how (e.g. musical performance), see *reading proficiency*.

Universal machine: See *Turing, Alan*. Further references are given in the Literature Appendix.

Watson, James: Together with Francis Crick, James Watson was the discoverer, in 1953, of the chemical structure of DNA, the substance that carries the hereditary properties of living organisms. Watson has told how the discovery was made in his book *The Double Helix*. This book is unique of its kind: an account of rare clarity, at first hand, of one of the greatest discoveries in the history of science.

   See also *foundations, scientific-scholarly activity*. Further references are given in the Literature Appendix.

Whitehead, Alfred North: See *mathematical logic*.

Wilkins, Maurice: See *scientific-scholarly activity*.

Will: The word 'will' enters into the philosophers' explanations of certain *–isms*. In ordinary conversation it is used commonly in various contexts. In certain situations one may question whether something done by a person was done wilfully. The situation is, for example, that the person has just been holding a dish, but that the dish has slipped out of the hands of the person, and fallen broken on the floor. It may then be meaningfully asked whether the person did it wilfully. But irrespective of the use of the word 'will' in this locution, it gives no indication that the person is equipped with a special organ, 'the will', which perhaps has been active. What we ask is whether the person in advance of the slipping of the dish has had a conscious intent that it should drop. What we enquire about is what thoughts the person has had. If the person has been thinking something in the direction of: 'now I let this dish crash on the floor', then we say that the person did it wilfully, otherwise we assign the fall of the dish to the clumsiness of the person.

   But the question whether the person did it wilfully makes sense only in situations when something undesirable has happened. If a person has put a dish in its proper place there can be no question of wilfulness. Claiming that we exercise our will at each action we perform is nonsense.

   We may also say that a person has a strong will. But again this does not refer to a special organ. The phrase is ordinarily taken to mean that the person in certain activities tends to make plans and to hold on to them, even when their realization meets opposition.

   To ask whether the will is free makes no sense. 'The will' does not denote something that may be free or bound.

Wittgenstein, Ludwig: Wittgenstein appears to be the present day Danish philosophers' man before anybody else. Thus Søren Kjørup spends a whole introductory column of his newspaper review of Wittgenstein's *Philosophische Untersuchungen* on indicating his importance before that of ten other philosophers.

   See *language, word-as-code-of-meaning-fallacy*.

Word-as-code-of-meaning-fallacy: By this will here be denoted a notion which is prominent with both laymen and philosophers, to the effect that each word is a *code of a meaning which is known by and common to those who talk with each other*. This notion is displayed every day in the language columns of newspapers and has been given striking expression by, among others, Einstein, Russell, and Wittgenstein.

Word-as-code-of-meaning-fallacy ...

Thus Einstein in *The Common Language of Science* says: 'If language is to lead at all to understanding, there must be ... a stable correspondence between signs and impressions.' Russell in *The Analysis of Mind,* p. 188, says: 'The word "Napoleon," we say, "means" a certain person. In saying this, we are asserting a relation between the word "Napoleon" and the person so designated. It is this relation that we must now investigate.'

In Wittgenstein the word-as-code-of-meaning-fallacy is displayed elaborately in the first pages of his *Philosophische Untersuchungen.* He opens his book by a quotation from Augustine's *Confessions* in which the latter tells about his childhood. The quotation is given by Wittgenstein in its original Latin form, to which the editor of Wittgenstein's text has added a German translation. This quotation in translation from the German version, but with addition of a few words from the original Latin form, is as follows:

'When the adults mentioned some thing and in doing so turned to it, I saw it and I understood that the thing was designated by the sound they uttered, since they wanted to refer to *it.* This I perceived from their gestures, the natural language (verbis naturalibus) of all people, which by the play of face and eyes, by the motions of the members and the tone of voice indicates the feelings of the soul, when it desires, or seizes, or rejects, or abhors something. So I gradually learned to understand which things were denoted by the words (verba) that I time after time heard pronounced in their definite places in various sentences.'

To this Wittgenstein says first:

'In these words we get, it seems to me, a definite picture of the essence of the human language. To wit: The words of the language denote things—sentences are combinations of such denotations.——In this picture of the language we find the root of the idea: Each word has a meaning. This meaning is assigned to the word. It is the thing the word stands for.'

In spite of its apparent clarity, this Wittgensteinian presentation is a school example of philosophical misinterpretation and obscurity. The philosophical destination appears when Wittgenstein pursues 'the essence of the human language', see *essence.*

Wittgenstein's misinterpretation of Augustine's account lies primarily where he says: 'In this picture of the language we find the root of the idea: Each word has a meaning.' But the word 'language' has come in by the translation. Augustine talks only about word, Latin 'verbum', and this to Augustine may be something spoken, but it may also be 'the play of face and eyes, the motions of the members and the tone of voice'.

Furthermore, Wittgenstein entirely ignores that which in Augustine's account is dominating, to wit that the meaning of words is something Augustine himself has acquired as habit, by time and time again experiencing the combination of the spoken word with that which the word denotes. In other words, Augustine explicitly describes the meaning of the words as residing in personal habits, while Wittgenstein distorts by claiming that Augustine supposedly says that the meaning of the words is given, 'exists' in the Aristotelian sense, independently of each person's individual, habitual understanding.

Pursuing this line Wittgenstein continues a page later with misleading and unclear talk:

'Let us think of a language which conforms to the description given by Augustine: The language will serve the mutual understanding of a mason A and a helper B. A erects a building of stones; there are bricks, columns, plates, and beams at hand. B has to hand him the stones, in the order in which A needs them. For this purpose they make use of a language consisting of the words: "brick", "column", "plate", "beam". A calls them out;—B brings the stone he has learnt to bring at this call.——Conceive this as a complete, primitive language.'

This is entirely misleading, first of all where Wittgenstein about the agreement between the two parties, A and B, being described, uses the designation 'a language which conforms to the description given by Augustine'. By using the designation 'a language' in this context Wittgenstein postulates that this agreement in some sense is analogous to ordinary linguistic activity, and thus gives expression to the *language-as-something-fallacy*.

Moreover Wittgenstein totally ignores Augustine's careful account of how his acquisition of the meaning of words has happened as a development of habits. Thus Wittgenstein describes a meaningless situation for A and B. He says that they 'make use of a language consisting of the words: "brick", "column", "plate", "beam"', which make out 'a complete, primitive language'. But how have they arrived at this? How has the mutual understanding of A and B about this come about, without they having been able to communicate in terms of many other words and signs, that have been exchanged in quite definite situations and contexts?

Wittgenstein's explanation of what is called the meaning of the words "brick", "column", "plate", and "beam" is unclear. He says that 'B brings the stone he has learnt to bring at this call'. But this explanation makes no sense in the context, since there is no definite stone that corresponds to any one of the words, e.g. "plate". What in fact happens, if the description is to make sense, is that B brings one of the stones under the designation called out by A. This means that A's call of the same word, e.g. "plate", in turn denotes ever different things, to wit, the plates lying ready, taken one by one. Thus Wittgenstein's own explanation, that each word means something definite, turn out to be wrong, even for what Wittgenstein calls 'a complete, primitive language'. It holds in the same way for the agreement between A and B described by Wittgenstein as for any other linguistic activity, that the words being used are understood only in each specific situation, and that the understanding of the same word may change from one moment to the next.

The fallacy of the philosophical claim of a fixed meaning for each word is brought out both in pronouncements by competent linguists and psychologists, and by simple considerations. Thus the following may be adduced:

(1) William James says in *Principles of Psychology*, vol. I, p. 472:
'When I use the word *man* in two different sentences, I may have both times exactly the same sound upon my lips and the same picture in my mental eye, but I may mean, and at the very moment of uttering the word and imagining the picture, know that I mean, two entirely different things. Thus when I say: "What a wonderful man Jones is!" I am perfectly aware that I mean by man to exclude Napoleon Bonaparte or Smith. But when I say: "What a wonderful thing Man is!" I am equally well aware that I mean to *in*clude not only Jones, but Napoleon and Smith as well. This added consciousness is an absolutely positive sort of feeling, transforming what would otherwise be mere noise or vision into something *understood;* and determining the sequel of my thinking, the later words and images, in a perfectly definite way.'

(2) The meaning of some of the most frequently used words, thus the pronouns, *she, he,* etc. and all the names, John, Sophie, Rosalind, William, etc., so obviously depends entirely upon the momentary situation in which they are used and the understanding of the person who says them and understands them, that it should be visible even to the dullest philosopher.

(3) The word-as-code-of-meaning-fallacy is rejected explicitly by Otto Jespersen, who in his book *Philosophy of Grammar*, p. 29, writes:

> 'My chief object in writing this chapter has been to make the reader realize that language is not exactly what a one-sided occupation with dictionaries and the usual grammars might lead us to think, but a set of habits, of habitual actions, and that each word and each sentence spoken is a complex action on the part of the speaker.'

What a dictionary can say about any word may (of course) explain only some of the aspects of the meaning of the word, to wit those that are *common to the use of the word in the texts upon which the dictionary builds.* When the word is used in a particular situation and linguistic context it will mean something specific that cannot be found in the dictionary.

When for example a person during an ordinary meal gathering says to a companion: 'Will you pass me the bread, please', then 'Will you' talks about precisely that companion and his or her willingness, 'pass' talks about the movement of the companion's arm here and now, 'me' denotes the person who is speaking now and no one else, and 'the bread' denotes, not a single piece of bread, but that basket with its contents of bread that at the moment of speech is located on the table. That 'the bread' has to be understood in this way (which is not explained in any dictionary) depends entirely on the understanding of the participating persons of the total situation in which it is pronounced, including both the specific meal situation and the words that come along with it, in particular 'pass'. That this is the case becomes clear as soon as we consider what 'the bread' would mean in other conversational contexts. If for example the person during the same meal said: 'The bread is not fresh', then 'the bread' presumably would denote, in the first place some of the bread that earlier had been placed in the basket but now had been eaten, and in the second place what is left in the basket, but not the basket itself.

If the request 'Will you pass me the bread, please' is made at a similar meal the day after, the word 'bread' probably will denote something else, perhaps another basket with other pieces of bread.

(4) Many words are used commonly to denote items that have nothing in common. This holds for example for 'pass'. Such words the dictionary explains by describing several different aspects of meaning side by side, so-called homonymy. That this does not raise any problem in ordinary speaking and writing is explained simply by the fact that the decisive part of the meaning is given only by the understanding of specific persons in a specific situation. Thus the two persons referred to above are aware that the word 'pass' in their meal situation denotes neither that something elapses, nor that somebody departs or dies. This they know because they have acquired such habits that 'pass', when said in a meal situation as the one sketched and as part of the request 'Will you pass me the bread, please', associates to (the thought of) the movement of the arm that will move the bread basket.

(5) The mental process taking place when a person understands a linguistic signal, in conversation or reading, is not different from the process taking place at *perception* of anything else. The linguistic signal, that is the spoken sound or the written text, in any case is merely a detail of what is heard or seen. As at any other perception, the linguistic signal is combined with the person's momentary thought object, and this totality by association calls forth a new thought object. The meaning the person may be said to assign to the linguistic signal then appears as part of that new thought object. Thus the meaning may embrace thoughts and feelings of any kind. The meaning of a linguistic signal will, like any other thought object, consist of an ephemeral multitude which is impossible to describe in its entirety. See *language, perception, stream of thought.*

(6) If the meaning of the words were given by a code any linguistic utterance would mean something definite. However, much of what is said or written with words, not the least what comes from philosophers, is nonsense, in that, in the context at hand, the denotations contained in them lack clear reference. See *–ism, artificial intelligence.*

(7) Where questions about the meaning of words is taken up in language philosophy the matter is shrouded in a mist. For example Chomsky in *Topics in the Theory of Generative Grammar* writes:

'If a generative grammar is to pair signals with semantic interpretations, then the theory of generative grammar must provide a general, language-independent means for representing the signals and semantic interpretations that are interrelated by the grammars of particular languages. This fact has been recognized since the origins of linguistic theory, and traditional linguistics made various attempts to develop theories of universal phonetics and universal semantics that might meet this requirement. Without going into any detail, I think it would be widely agreed that the general problem of universal phonetics is fairly well understood ... whereas the problems of universal semantics still remain veiled in their traditional obscurity.'

In this passage 'signals' stand for what otherwise is called words, 'semantic interpretations' for meanings, and 'the signals and semantic interpretations that are interrelated' express what here is denoted word-as-code-of-meaning. But it does not occur to Chomsky that the phrase 'semantic interpretations' denotes nothing clearly. Rather, he makes it the starting point of his theory of generative grammars (see *language-rule-fallacy*), which thus builds on what he himself says is veiled in traditional obscurity.

Instead of the word-as-code-of-meaning-fallacy may be put:

(1) Speech activity is something personal, individual.

(2) A person's acquaintance with a certain word consists in the person's habit of perceiving the corresponding sound as a speech signal.

(3) That which may be called *a person's understanding of a linguistic utterance* has meaning only in relation to a specific situation in which the utterance enters.

(4) This understanding consists of the *thought object* that by virtue of the person's habitual associations momentarily is produced in the person's stream of thought when the person perceives the utterance in the situation.

See also *belief, concept.* Further references are given in the Literature Appendix.

World: The word enters into the philosophers' explanations of certain *–isms* (q.v.), but outside of definite contexts it designates nothing.

World of science: See *reality*.

Zinkernagel Peter: See *existence, language-as-something-fallacy, mathematical logic*.

Zoology: See *philosophy of science*.

Summary

For two thousand years, since Aristotle, the philosophers have presumed to possess the highest insight into the constitution of the world. They have encroached upon us with their talk of truth, logic, reality, essence, and being. Thereby they have perverted the understanding of human thinking and speech. They have imputed to us a barren, logic-bound conception of science and scholarship.

Antiphilosophical Dictionary displays the inanity of the traditional ways of talking of philosophers, as they are found in the writings of, among others, Descartes, Bertrand Russell, Gilbert Ryle, Martin Heidegger, and Ludwig Wittgenstein.

The main scientific contribution of the Dictionary is a coherent understanding of thinking, speech, and science/scholarship, that builds upon William James's classical description of the stream of thought and upon linguistic and scientific/scholarly practice as described by, among others, Otto Jespersen and James Watson. This understanding is presented, primarily, in the form of a set of articles explaining a particular use of the following descriptive terms:

> association, association by similarity, attention, belief, building site metaphor, concept, definition, description, description form, disposition, explanation, feeling, fringe, habit, introspection, knowhow, knowing, knowing by acquaintance, mental object, mind, model, octopus in pile of rags metaphor, perception, property, psychology, reasoning, scientific-scholarly activity, splashes over the waves metaphor, stream of consciousness, stream of thought, substantive state, thought, thought object, theory, thing, thinking, transitive state.

Additionally, the understanding of speech is presented in articles discussing 6 language-fallacies:

> concept-is-word-fallacy, understand-fallacy, word-as-code-of-meaning-fallacy, language-as-something-fallacy, language-rule-fallacy, thinking-as-language-fallacy.

The articles discuss and justify the way the descriptive terms should be used so as to achieve coherent descriptions of thinking, speech, and science/scholarship. The articles are interrelated to such an extent that no linear ordering of them can be preferred to any other. Accordingly they are ordered alphabetically by key word.

These articles are supplemented with other relevant articles, some of them explaining why certain terms are useless in describing thinking, speech, and science/scholarship.

The presentation form, articles discussing descriptive terms arranged alphabetically by term, is an independent scientific contribution, a particular description form suitable for describing a set of terms suitable for describing mental activities. This description form implies a deliberate rejection of the logical-philosophical form of presentation, which according to the view of science/scholarship presented is inadequate in the context.

Dansk resumé

I to tusind år, siden Aristoteles, har filosofferne påberåbt sig den højeste indsigt i verdens beskaffenhed. De har plaget os med deres bedrevidende snak om sandhed, logik, virkelighed, essens, og væren. Dermed har de forkvaklet forståelsen af menneskers tænkning og sproglighed. De har påduttet os en gold, logikbunden opfattelse af videnskabelighed.

I Antifilosofisk Leksikon afsløres forvrøvletheden i filosoffernes traditionelle talemåder, som de træffes hos bl.a. Descartes, Bertrand Russell, Gilbert Ryle, Martin Heidegger, og Ludwig Wittgenstein.

Det videnskabelige hovedbidrag i Leksikon er en sammenhængende opfattelse af tænkning, sproglighed, og videnskabelighed, der bygger på William James klassiske beskrivelse af tankestrømmen og på sproglig og videnskabelig praksis som beskrevet af bl.a. Otto Jespersen og James Watson. Denne opfattelse fremlægges primært i form af en samling af artikler der gør rede for en bestemt måde at anvende følgende beskrivende termer:

association, association by similarity, attention, belief, building site metaphor, concept, definition, description, description form, disposition, explanation, feeling, fringe, habit, introspection, knowhow, knowing, knowing by acquaintance, mental object, mind, model, octopus in pile of rags metaphor, perception, property, psychology, reasoning, scientific-scholarly activity, splashes over the waves metaphor, stream of consciousness, stream of thought, substantive state, thought, thought object, theory, thing, thinking, transitive state.

Dertil fremlægges opfattelsen af sproglighed i artikler der drøfter 6 sprogvildfarelser:

concept-is-word-fallacy, understand-fallacy, word-as-code-of-meaning-fallacy, language-as-something-fallacy, language-rule-fallacy, thinking-as-language-fallacy.

Artiklerne drøfter og begrunder den måde de beskrivende termer skal anvendes for at etablere sammenhængende beskrivelser af tænkning, sproglighed, og videnskabelighed. Artiklerne hænger sammen i en sådan grad at ingen lineær ordning af dem kan foretrækkes frem for nogen anden. De er derfor ordnet alfabetisk efter nøgleord.

Disse artikler suppleres med andre relevante artikler, hvoraf visse forklarer hvorfor visse termer er ubrugelige til at beskrive tænkning, sproglighed, og videnskabelighed.

Præsentationsformen, artikler der drøfter beskrivende termer, ordnet alfabetisk efter term, er et uafhængig videnskabeligt bidrag, en bestemt beskrivelsesform, der er egnet til at beskrive en samling termer der egner sig til at beskrive mentale aktiviteter. Denne beskrivelsesform indebærer en udtrykkelig forkastelse af den logisk-filosofiske form for præsentation, der i følge det syn på videnskabelighed der fremlægges er uegnet i sammenhængen.

Literature Appendix

Supplementary discussions of the issues of the dictionary may be found in other of my writings, as follows:

Naur, P.: 1992, *Computing: A Human Activity*. ACM Press/Addison Wesley, Reading, Mass.

Some of the chapters in this book supplement the discussions of the dictionary, as shown below by references from the keywords of the dictionary:

1.3. Programming Languages, Natural Languages, and Mathematics: *mathematical analysis, programming language.*

1.5. Computing and the So–Called Foundations of the So–Called Sciences: *foundations (of sciences), law of nature, model, program control, science.*

5.2. Proof of Algorithms by General Snapshots: *logic.*

7.1. Formalization in Program Development: *formal language, programming language.*

7.5. The Place of Strictly Defined Notation in Human Insight: *logic.*

8.1. The Electronic Computer and the Brain: *artificial intelligence, program control.*

8.2. Thinking and Turing's Test: *artificial intelligence, Alan Turing.*

8.3. Review of D. Michie: Machine Intelligence and Related Topics: *artificial intelligence.*

8.4. Programming Languages Are Not Languages—Why 'Programming Language' Is a Misleading Designation: *formal language, language, programming language, word-as-code-of-meaning-fallacy.*

8.5. Review of Y. Shoham: Reasoning About Change: Time and Causation From the Standpoint of Artificial Intelligence: *artificial intelligence.*

8.6. Causes and Human Expectations and Intents: *cause.*

Naur, P.: 1995, *Knowing and the Mystique of Logic and Rules*, Kluwer Academic Publishers, xii + 365 pp..

Some of the chapters in this book supplement the discussions of the dictionary, as shown below by references from the keywords of the dictionary:

1.1. William James's Psychology of Knowing: *association by similarity, attention, belief, feeling, habit, introspection, William James, knowing, perception, psychology, reality, reasoning, stream of thought, thinking-as-language-fallacy, thought-as-perception-mistake.*

As a standard source of what philosophers consider philosophy to be I have used:
Dictionary of Philosophy, Runes, D. D. (red.) with 72 co-authors, Littlefield, Adams, New Jersey, 1962, 343 s.

The quotations and discussions of the dictionary additionally refer to the following sources:

Austin, J. L.: 1946, 'Other Minds', in *Logic and Language*, 2nd series, A. Flew (ed.), Blackwell, Oxford, 1953, pp. 123-158.
Ayer, A. J.: 1956, *The Problem of Knowledge*, Penguin, London.
Chomsky, N.: 1971, *Topics in the Theory of Generative Grammar*, in *The Philosophy of Language*, J. R. Searle (ed.), Oxford Univ. Press.
Chomsky, N.: 1972, *Language and Mind*, Harcourt Brace Jovanovich, San Diego, California.
Descartes, R.: 1637, *Discours sur la Methode*.
Eddington, A.: 1928, *The Nature of the Physical World*, Cambridge Univ. Press.
Einstein, A.: 1921, *Über die spezielle und die allgemeine Relativitätstheorie*, Vieweg, Braunschweig.
Einstein, A.: 1934, 'On the Method of Theoretical Physics', in *The World As I See It*, Convici Friede, New York.
Einstein, A.: 1941, 'The Common Language of Science', 1936, 'Physics and Reality', 1940, The Fundaments of Theoretical Physics, in *Out of My Later Years*, Philosophical Library, New York.

Encyclopædia Britannica, Fifteenth Edition: 1991, Chicago.

Farrington, B.: 1953, *Greek Science*, Penguin.

Hartnack, J.: 1957, *Filosofiske essays*, Gyldendal.

Heidegger, M.: 1986, *Sein und Zeit*, Niemeyer, Tübingen.

James, W.: 1890, *The Principles of Psychology*, Henry Holt, USA; reprinted in Dover, 1950.

Jespersen, O.: 1924, *The Philosophy of Grammar*, George Allen and Unwin, London.

Jespersen, O.: 1933, *Essentials of English Grammar*, George Allen and Unwin, London.

Kuhn, T. S.: 1970, *The Structure of Scientific Revolutions,* 2nd enlarged edition, Univ. of Chicago Press, Chicago, Illinois.

Newton, I.: 1686, *Philosophiae Naturalis Principia Mathematica.*

Poincaré, H.: 1913, 'Mathematical Creation', in *The World of Mathematics*, J. R. Newman (Ed.), Simon and Schuster, New York, 1956.

Popper, K. R.: 1959, *The Logic of Scientific Discovery*, 10th impression, Hutchinson, London, 1980.

Popper, K. R.: 1963, *Conjectures and Refutations*, Routledge and Kegan Paul, London.

Quine, W. V.: 1987, *Quiddities*, Harvard Univ. Press.

Quine, W. V.: 1960, *Word and Object*, M. I. T. Press, Cambridge, Mass.

Russell, B.: 1912, 'On the Notion of Cause', 'Knowledge by Acquaintance and Knowledge by Description', in *Mysticism and Logic*, Penguin, London, 1953.

Russell, B.: 1921, *The Analysis of Mind*, George Allen and Unwin, London.

Russell, B.: 1919, *Introduction to Mathematical Philosophy*, George Allen and Unwin, London.

Russell, B., Whitehead, A. N.: 1910, *Principia Mathematica,* Cambridge Univ. Press.

Ryle, G.: 1932, 'Systematically Misleading Expressions', in *Logic and Language*, 2nd series, A. Flew (Ed.), Blackwell, Oxford, 1953, pp. 11-36.

Ryle, G.: 1949, *The Concept of Mind*, Penguin, London.

Turing, A. M.: 1937/37, 'On Computable Numbers, With an Application to the Entscheidungsproblem',*Proc. London Math. Soc.* ser. 2, vol. 42, pp. 230-265.

Turing, A.: Computing Machinery and Intelligence. *Mind* LIX, 236 (1950), 433-460; also in Newman, J. R. (Ed.) *The World of Mathematics Vol. 4.* Simon and Schuster, New York, 1956, pp. 2099-2133.

Watson, J.: 1968, *The Double Helix,* Signet, New York.

Wittgenstein, L.: 1971, *Philosophische Untersuchungen,* Suhrkamp.